mac
tips
AND
TRICKS

Prima Publishing, Rocklin, CA 95677-1260

Printed in Spain

Text and design copyright © Carlton Books Limited 1994

Library of Congress Cataloging-in-Publication Data is available on request

ISBN 1-55958-537-4

Prima Publishing, Inc., has made every effort to determine that the information contained in this book is accurate. However, the publisher makes no warranty, either expressed or implied, as to the accuracy, effectiveness, or completeness of the material in this book; nor does the publisher assume liability for damages, either incidental or consequential, that may result from using the information in this book. The publisher cannot provide information regarding hardware or software. Questions should be directed to the support numbers provided by the software and device manufacturers in their documentation.

Project Editor: Tim Smith
Project Art Direction: Fiona Knowles
Production Controller: Garry Lewis

mac tips

AND

TRICKS

Caroline Bassett & Guy Sneesby

P

PRIMA

Contents

Introduction

There are those for whom information technology and hardcore computing are interesting in themselves. They're prepared to work at it. They have t-shirts with slogans from strange software companies. They like code.

Then there's the rest of us. We buy computers because they are useful tools.

We hope they will make our lives simpler and more efficient, at home, at work, or at school, but we don't enjoy wading through manuals. In short, we've got lives to live. We want the results, without the effort.

If you've bought a Mac, you've already made your first good move – its the friendliest personal computer on the planet, and it's also very consistent, so any tricks you learn in one Mac applications will prove just as indispensible in another.

This book is for Mac users who want to learn to process words, to use a database to organize their lives, to design pages, to use graphics and even get into multimedia – in other words to achieve the tasks they bought their Macs for in the first place, without going mad in the process.

We've stuck to the absolute basics. The early chapters of this book explain how the Mac system operates; in later chapters you'll learn how to get under the hood of your Mac, to customize it to the way you like it; and finally you'll learn how to work quickly and effectively with applications. If you're feeling confident, you can skip over the early chapters and go straight to the application section you're interested in.

Macs are full of shortcuts for speedy users. The most crucial key on the Mac is the Command key – its the one with the Apple on it (in fact it appears twice on most keyboards with one key on each side of the space bar). This is the key that lets you navigate effortlessly around your Mac without dragging your mouse through thousands of sub-menus. Combine it with other keys to Open, Close, Save and Quit documents and do virtually any other job on the Mac. This is the key that expresses an ideal relationship between human and machine – you use it to make your Mac work for you, not the other way around.

Caroline and Guy

Author biographies:

Caroline Bassett is the editor of one of Europe's leading Macintosh monthlies in the form of *MacUser UK*; having worked her way up via the posts of News Editor and Deputy Editor on the same title.

Her professional Mac-using experience came in crashing Macs as a copy and production editor in the intense environment of the weekly computer industry journal, *MicroScope*.

She is an English Literature Graduate – (and therefore human??), a Scuba diver (therefore lazy – all you do is sink), also proud but bitter (they cut the prices) owner of an utterly standard Macintosh LC... luckily she is also in receipt of the key to the *MacUserUK* labs...

If you want to get in touch via email the address is caroline@cix.compulink.co.uk

Guy Sneesby graduated in engineering at Liverpool Polytechnic in 1986. Since then he has worked as a journalist, first as a reporter and then as the editor of a monthly computer systems newspaper called *Microsystem Design*. For the last two years he has been at *MacUser UK*, one of Europe's leading Macintosh magazines, as news editor. Having shown his worth there, he was promoted to edit a brand new magazine – *CD-ROM Magazine* – which is planned to explore and detail the cutting edge of the new computer medium.

Thanks to Paul at Blueeyedog for the video, Ian, Stuart, Karen and the rest of the MU codeheads. They know who they are.

● ●

Kickstart Your Mac

The Absolute Hardware Basics

1

The Mac is easy to use. It's easy to set up. It's easy to start working with... at least that's what the advertizing would have us believe. So what happens when you get behind the 'Easy' bits, what does the actual set up of your Mac mean, and how do you get the most of out it once you've got that first screen blinking away at you? Find out right here...

Get Port-abled

It is useful to know which icon is which when you're trying to work out which part to plug into which port ('ports' are computerspeak for sockets). Get the lowdown here...

ADB PORT: ADB stands for Apple Desktop Bus. The ADB socket at the back of your Mac is for the keyboard (and a number of other devices that we'll talk about later). You can 'daisy-chain' your mouse to your Mac through the keyboard as the ADB icons at either end of the keyboard indicate. Left-handers will be pleased to know it makes no difference which side of the keyboard you slot in the mouse. Switch off before you switch sides though.

SOUND OUTPUT PORT: Every Mac has an audio output port. It can be used with standard plugs – like the kind on personal stereos. Remember, this is for output only, it isn't where to connect your microphone, if you have one.

SOUND INPUT PORT: Your microphone cable slots into a hole that's labelled like this. Don't mix this up with the output port – Apple says you could damage your equipment if you connect your output device to it.

VIDEO PORT: The video port looks like a TV – naturally enough it's where you connect your monitor or screen.

MODEM PORT: This is for a modem if you have one. You can also link up a printer through this port because, like the printer port, it is a simple 'Serial' socket.

PRINTER PORT: This one's self-evident – although you don't have to link your printer up here; you can use the modem port if you want to. (To find out how, see the section on the Chooser in Chapter 3.)

SCSI PORT: The SCSI (pronounced 'scuzzy') port at the back of every Mac enables different devices to be connected to your system. These include some types of printers, extra hard drives and CD-ROM players.

SCSI is useful because it enables up to seven SCSI devices to be connected to each other in a long string (or daisychain). Every SCSI device has an adjustable number between 0 and 7, and each device in any single chain must take a different number. If two devices have the same 'identity' they could clash – or 'conflict' in Macspeak – and you could lose data.

Your Mac has the number 7 and your internal hard drive has the number 0. So if you need to add a device don't choose these numbers. (To find out more see Chapter 12.)

GETTING GOING

Once your Mac is cabled up you're ready to go. Some machines will need to be turned on via a switch at the back; others will use a far more convenient switch at the top of the keyboard.

THE SYSTEM

 System software is the operations manager that runs your Mac. It's only installed once and from then on resides on the hard disk of your machine. Most cheaper Macs come with system software already loaded up these days. Assuming this is the case, when you switch on you'll get this 'Happy Mac' screen followed by the Desktop.

 If there are problems, you'll probably see a small picture (this is an 'icon' in Macspeak) of a disk with a question mark blinking in a rather annoying way at the center of the screen. This means your Mac can't find system software. Reinstalling it should fix this. To reinstall the system go to the system disks that came with your Mac, put the first disk in and follow the on-screen instructions. If you have a Performa and no system disks were included with your machine, you'll have to contact the people you bought it from and obtain a new set. It was one of Apple's cheaper decisions not to include them on the basis that people should make their own back ups.

CUSTOM INSTALL

Your Mac may ask you if you wish to custom install your software – that is, be selective about which parts of the software you load. It's wise to put everything on at first. Leave customizing until you know what you want and are familiar with your Mac.

WHICH SYSTEM AND WHICH MAC?

System software has different version numbers depending on when it was developed. Unless your Mac is very old you need to be using the most recent version of System 7 – older versions of system software, for example System 6, may work but you can't do as much with them. New applications are built to work with – that is, be compatible with – modern systems.

The vast majority of Macs bought and sold in the last few years are fitted with System 7. This book is designed to help new Mac owners using comparatively modern machines to quickly become productive and even advanced in the use of their Macs. As such it has been planned with System 7 very much in mind.

This is not to say that people with older machines that run System 6 can't get anything from this book. Apple's evolutionary approach to improving the system means that many of today's applications and utilities, and some of the tricks of the trade, work on every kind of Mac.

However the significant progress Apple has made with System 7 inevitably means that many of the features outlined in this book will simply not be available on machines that have System 6, or earlier systems, installed.

WORKING WITH PERFORMAS: BEAT THE SYSTEM

Macintosh Performas, which run a slightly altered version of System 7 called System 7.xP – x denotes the upgrade number – also have number of features and a few idiosyncrasies not evident on 'standard' Macs.

To find out what system your Mac is using, first click on your hard disk or any other standard desktop icon, or select Finder from the application menu at the top right-hand corner of your screen, to take you to back to the desktop.

Next click on the Apple icon at the top left-hand side of the screen and select About This Macintosh from the pull down menu.

As you can see from the picture below, this Mac is running System 1-7.1P.

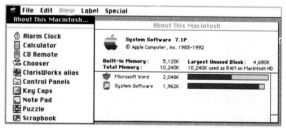

Finding out about your Mac system is a case of click and look.

The figure 7.1 indicates that this is an advanced version of System 7 with a few minor added features. These will become particularly evident when it comes to handling fonts. More about this in Chapter 6.

The letter P denotes that the machine is a Performa. This is something you couldn't fail to have noticed when you bought your machine. It says Macintosh Performa and, when it boots up (this terminology is taken from the phrase 'to pull yourself up by your own bootstraps'), it will display two features that are unique to Performas and, in many people's view, entirely unnecessary for the majority of users.

These features are intended to make Mac Performas even easier to use than Macs. However, the unfortunate by-product is that it makes them different, which can mean that skills painfully learned using Performas don't easily transfer to the majority of 'standard' machines.

At Ease is a simplified interface, designed to enable very young children or occasional users to launch and use applications without first having to master the Mac. It consists of two folders: Applications and Documents. These can be configured to limit other people's access to only a predetermined range of files. There is also a basic password protection system built in to prevent people from accidentally – or maliciously – trashing data.

The Launcher is an application launch pad that enables a limited number of applications to be launched with a single click on a configurable set of big friendly buttons. Again it is a tool that would typically be set up by a more experienced user for occasional use by young children or out-and-out greenhorns.

If you feel these features would be useful to you, leave them activated and read more about configuring them in the comprehensive At Ease manual and the User's Guide that came with your Mac.

Fortunately, it is possible to switch off At Ease and Launcher to make your Performa very like a standard Mac and, unless you have a specific requirement for these features, it is advisable that you do so.

To switch off At Ease, double click on the hard disk, and then on the Control Panels folder inside. Double click on the control panel icon labelled At Ease, and the panel shown below will appear. Simply click the At Ease switch to the Off position and that's all there is to it.

To permanently switch off the Launcher, first double click on your hard disk icon, and then on the System Folder you find inside. Inside the System Folder, click on the Startup Items folder, and drag the Launcher

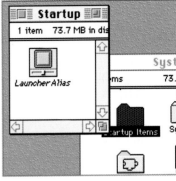

Launcher: great at first, then a pain.

Alias (more about Aliases later) item to the Trash. You can easily create another alias if you ever need to.

Finally, select Restart from the pull down Special Menu and your Mac will Shut Down and boot up again with pretty much the look and feel of an ordinary Mac.

There are one or two other minor differences to overcome, but these will be explained as and when they crop up in later chapters.

DESKTOP OR FINDER?

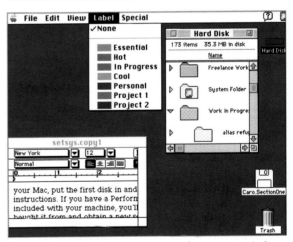

The Desktop, your working environment, is yours to control.

You are Here. This is the Desktop. Strictly speaking, the Desktop is what you see. The Finder is the part of the system software that puts it on screen (and does a great deal else as well, as we'll see later). However, it's OK to use the two terms interchangeably – many people do, since the Finder and its Desktop metaphor are inextricably linked.

Take a quick look at your screen. You'll see a long bar running along the top – the menu bar – and, as the name suggests, this gives you a wide range of options. Pull-down menus – and even pull-down pull-down menus (sub menus) – give you many more choices.

The Desktop's menu bar will become a second home to you.
Below that, on the Desktop itself, is an icon. Icons are small pictures representing different folders, files, applications or drives. Mac users with time on their hands acquire the software to spend hours and hours customizing these icons. Some of you may feel this is analogous to stencilling go-faster stripes onto your roller skates – if you've bought a second-hand machine, and flying toasters erupt onto your screen every so often, it may mean your Desktop has already been customized to some extent.

In this case the icon is a hard disk, the place where files, applications and system information are stored on your Mac. It will probably be labeled as such. Clicking it will open up a window that will list either by icon or by name, all the files and applications currently stored on this particular hard disk.

Directly below in the bottom right-hand corner is the Trash (in UK versions, this is called the Wastebasket). You can make use of the Trash to dispose of unwanted files and, although you can get them back (see Chapter 2 to find out how) it's best to regard them as permanently disposed of. The Trash becomes swollen when it has some trash in it.

THE FINDER

The Desktop operates as a kind of basecamp and Apple has wisely made sure you can always find it. In the top right-hand corner of your desktop is a Mac icon. That's the Finder icon. You won't always see it. When you are working in an application you'll see the application icon displayed, but (as we've mentioned) clicking in this area will always navigate you to the Desktop. Here's how…

Below we're in Microsoft *Word* – a popular word processing application. Looking at the top right-hand

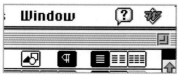

corner of the screen, you will see a discrete *Word* icon in the same positon that the Finder icon (a small Mac) used to be…

Notice that the Finder icon (top right) has changed to the *Word* icon.

…clicking with the mouse on the *Word* icon brings up a list of different activities and areas – including the Mac icon that symbolizes the Finder.

Dragging the mouse (keep holding it down) down to

Don't Panic! Get back to base with a simple pull-down and click.

the Finder icon and releasing when it is selected will take you back to the Desktop. This is true wherever you are. (You can return to your original place, in this case back to *Word*, in the same way)

Notice that the other items on the menu bar running along the top of the window change depending on which application you are in.

The Desktop is your first taste of the Mac's famous Graphical User Interface – GUI (pronounced 'goo-ee'). The Mac GUI is supposed to be intuitive enough to use, even if you are as drunk as a skunk, with the lights off. A first glance at the screen may not confirm that impression, but you'll find the Mac is easy, once you take a little time to learn how it works.

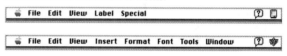

The Finder icon – now you see it (top) now you don't (bottom).

DEFINING YOUR OWN HOME

It's now time for some definitions. We'll start with the System software. Your Mac uses System software to start itself up, to run applications, and it controls the Finder which enables you to navigate between everything. The System is, therefore, the soul of the Mac.

Your System software is organized into a single System folder on installation. Be careful with it – even if you rename everything else on your desktop after your favourite sports team, or your pet dog, it makes sense to stick with an easily indentifiable name for the System folder. As the illustration above shows, it looks distinctive too.

System Folder

If you click on the system folder you'll see that there are many different icons within it that control different aspects of the way your Mac works. Some of the files in the system folder won't be familiar, but be wary of discarding files from it; they may be placed there automatically when you install applications. And they may be necessary to your Mac-life.

Kickstart Your Mac

Applications (or 'Apps' as power users call them) are at the core of your future Mac productivity.

Now for 'Applications'. Also called 'Programs'. These are pieces of software designed to perform particular tasks; for example to process words, draw pictures, manipulate data including figures and charts. The picture left shows icons from a few popular programs. The aim is that these icons are distinctive enough to indicate the nature of the application – *Kid Pix*, for example, is a children's paint package.

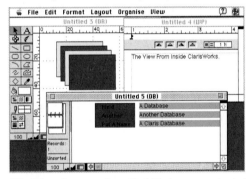

'Works' packages such as *ClarisWorks* are popular today.

Some applications software is now designed to do a number of jobs – these packages are called 'Works' packages – and are often sold alongside, or as a part of, the deal with Macs, particularly Performas. The picture above shows three open windows running different aspects of *ClarisWorks*: a drawing, word processing and databasing module. Each one of these elements uses tools that will become familiar as we go on with the book. For example, the tool palette on the far left in the draw package includes different brushes, a paint-bucket and different pen choices; the word processing document includes a ribbon with tab and format options; and the database includes a tool to show how many records there are.

Every Mac is sold with a free application included. This is called *TeachText* and it is a very, very basic word processor. It isn't good enough for complex work, you'll need your own word processing software for that.

'File' (or 'Document'): this is your work. Again it may consist of words, pictures, moving pictures, or a mixture of these media. If you're using a word processing application, your document comprizes the words of your best-seller; if you're using a paint package, your file or document is the masterpiece that the world has been waiting for.

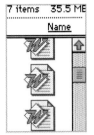

Once you've grasped the difference between these three file types, you'll race through the Mac basics. To recap: there's controlling System software; there's Application software which enables you to perform a specific task; and there are Documents or Files, which are the products of your work.

Document icons reflect the package they were created in – as the shot above of Microsoft *Word* files shows. There is one more icon you'll see as you take a first look

at your new electronic domain; a Folder is a place in which to gather together related files – as you would in a file cabinet. You can place applications or documents in different folders and move them around simply by dragging. You'll see when you launch your Mac that your System is already in a folder. Make sure you know the difference between a folder and document or you could be in for some confusion. (See Chapter 2 on the Finder for more about using folders.)

You'll notice that clicking with the mouse on any of these items on the desktop highlights them, while double clicking 'launches' them – that's to say it makes them open. If you highlight a file (click on it) while keeping your finger down on your mouse you can drag it around the desktop. This way you can build your desktop to suit yourself. You can change the size of windows and recolor the background of your desktop too. (More about customizing your Desktop in Chapter 2.)

That's the Desktop at a glance. If you've had enough theory and you want to do something really useful you'll need to know one more fact – how to turn your Mac off.

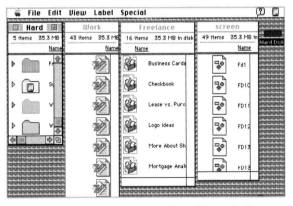

A particularly gaudy-looking desktop, but still a workable one.

SWITCHING OFF

In Macspeak, turning off your Mac in order to save on the electricity bill is known as 'Powering Down'. Doing this is simpler; move the mouse over to the Special category in the menu bar running across the top of your Desktop. Now choose the Shut Down option by highlighting it in the pull-down menu that appears if you drag your mouse down the menu bar (keep the mouse button depressed). Release the button to take up this end-of-the-day option. The Mac will automatically ask you what to do with any documents you've left unsaved (or open) and will then close down. It is now safe to switch off your Mac, as the message box tells you (if it hasn't done so automatically). That's it, or almost it. If you decide that closing down wasn't what you really wanted to do after all, you can choose Restart by clicking on the Restart button or switching back on. Remember, though, this won't help if you had work and didn't save it – you'll have lost it already. Save before you close down.

Don't feel you have to turn your Mac off when you're taking short breaks. It can look after itself. However, remember to save your work by selecting Save from the pull-down menu bars before leaving your Mac alone. (The exact location of the Save option may change, but you'll find a Save function in every application.) If you are going to leave your Mac alone for longer periods (say more than half an hour) it makes sense to close down your machine simply to save power.

One thing you shouldn't do however, is to leave your monitor on and unused for long periods. The reason for this is that the phosphors used to display the screen image could, theoretically, 'burn-in' the image you've left there. This has the potential to leave ghost marks on the screen. In our experience you have to leave a screen on a long, long time for anything of the sort to happen.

But this hasn't stopped many Mac users buying 'Screen Savers'. These programs serve two functions. First, they stop phosphor burn in by putting mobile on to your screen. Screen savers are also a way of customizing your Mac and make staring into space when you're stuck for words, less boring. The debate about the worth of screen savers still rages on however.

Power Tips . . . .

MOUSE TACTICS: manuals talk about mouse tactics for pages but it's best just to use your mouse until you get the feel for it. A hint: your mouse does not run out of space. If you're trying to get somewhere and you reach the edge of your mouse mat, keep the mouse button firmly depressed, lift up your mouse and move it back to where you began. Manoeuvring a mouse can make you feel ridiculous. Don't despair. The mouse is not a natural input metaphor, although it's better than text-based systems, and you'll get the hang of it very quickly.

POINT, CLICK: remember, point to what you want, click to select. Point to what you want, then double click to do. If you want to select two files at once, select with the shift key down (a useful trick called Shift-Select).

If the cursor moves too quickly you can alter the parameters dictating how responsive your mouse is, using the Mouse file in Control Panels under the Apple Menu. (See Chapter 3, to find out how).

TO LAUNCH AN APPLICATION: to open a document, you can click on its icon. But it may be quicker to click directly onto your document. This will launch the program for you.

SAVE AND WORK: your Mac hard disk is where you park your applications and files when you switch off your machine. Your hard disk retains information permanently – when you save you save onto your hard disk. You can do this when a file is still open. Save and Keep Working.

Drive-Ins

If you have an external hard drive (these don't come as standard with any Mac, so you'll know if you do) remember to turn this on a few seconds before you turn on the Mac itself. If you don't, the Mac won't 'see' it and you'll need to Restart before you can access it – reach it – from your machine.

Kickstart Your Mac

MEMORY AND STORAGE

If you don't understand how storage and memory work on the Mac, you will lose work because you'll never really be sure exactly what state your files are in. Sorting out how different forms of memory operate on a Mac should make it clear why you really, really need to save your work often – and why it makes sense to back up.

Like other personal computers, Macs have two kinds of memory – RAM or Random Access Memory and ROM or Read-Only Memory. Macs also have hard and floppy disks which are sometimes called memory by people who don't have the faintest idea about how computers work.

ROM is the stuff carved in silicon that makes the Mac Mac-like. Your Mac can read information engraved on to the ROMS but it can't change it. These ROMS are Apple's prize asset and are hidden away inside the Mac.

Read-Only effectively means you also can't make any alterations to this media – if you could get to it. And frankly there is no need for you to do this. Mac ROMs contain the core of your Mac, without them, you would be stuck with a lump of plastic.

RAM is a different matter. The amount of RAM you have dictates the brain power of your Mac.

How do you know what you've got? All Macs come configured with a certain amount of active memory and a certain amount of storage – if you buy a Mac LCIII 8/120, for example, you have 8 megabytes (we'll call it Mb from now on) of RAM. This enables you to juggle with applications, run them and temporarily store changes to documents you are working on.

The amount of RAM you have dictates the number of applications you can use at any one time and the speed at which they will run. RAM is short-term memory.

Storage is something else. In our example you have 120Mb of magnetic medium-type storage space to keep work you want to save on a permanent basis.

HOW MUCH ACTIVE RAM?

Go to the Desktop (make sure you've gor the Finder icon showing in the top right-hand corner) and click on the Apple menu (the Apple sign) at the left of your screen. The first entry will say About This Mac. Mouse down and release when it's highlighted. This will bring up a screen showing how much RAM your Mac contains – and how much is available. In our example, not very much – this machine came with 4Mb of RAM and we've

used up most of it just to run the System software. The rest is for and two applications. Notice that *Word*, a large application, is taking up over 2Mb while *TeachText* is grabbing very little.

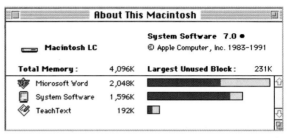

Your Mac is clever with its use of RAM, but it only has so much.

It is relatively simple to add more RAM to your Mac by adding more chips, or SIMMs (Single Inline Memory Modules) as they are known (It is wise to ask a dealer to do this. You could do it yourself if you follow instructions precisely, but it will void your warranty).

STORE IT!

Computer information is generally stored in much the same way as information is stored on music cassettes – that is, on magnetic media that can be erased and used again and again. This storage space may be inside your Mac – on your internal hard disk – or externally on less powerful (but still useful) floppy disks.

The big difference between your hard disk and a floppy disk is size – a floppy holds 1.4Mb of data maximum. An internal drive will hold 20Mb minimum – enough to hold over 400 pages of text but only a few comparatively small applications. However, a 20Mb hard disk really is small, you'll probably going to be looking at 130Mb as a minimum. There are other differences, too. Floppies are portable, but not they are not as robust as hard disks. The access times (the time is takes to read and write data) will be slower too.

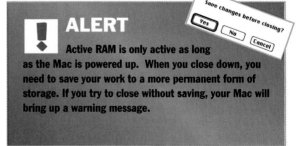

ALERT

Active RAM is only active as long as the Mac is powered up. When you close down, you need to save your work to a more permanent form of storage. If you try to close without saving, your Mac will bring up a warning message.

Here, reading along the title bar of a floppy disk, and the line below it, the amount already on the disk and the amount available on this floppy can be added together. They come to 1,416K or 1.4Mb – this is a 'high-density double-sided' disk. Normal double-sided disks hold less.

Caro.SectionOne			
3 items	839K in disk		577K available
Name	Size	Label	Last Modified
▷ ☐ copy for carlton	– –		Mon, Sep 20, 1993, 3:49 am
▷ ☐ KS screen shots	– –		Mon, Sep 20, 1993, 4:06 am
▷ ☐ m screen shots	– –		Mon, Sep 20, 1993, 4:06 am

Even a humble floppy can store very useful information.

LAUNCHING APPLICATIONS AND SAVING WORK

All this technical stuff is all very well, but suppose you actually want to do something useful – and then save it.

First you'll need to launch an application. Every Mac sold comes with *TeachText*, a simple word processing program. Most Performas will also come with some kind of multi-program *Works* package included in the price. So try launching any of these you find on your Mac.

 The *TeachText* icon looks like this.Once an application is installed, launching it is a double click away. Find the icon representing it, and double click on it with the mouse.

The application opens into a window. Notice the application has its own menu bar – it doesn't, for example, look like the one that runs across the Finder.

🍎 **File Edit**	⑦ ◈
Untitled	
Welcome to TeachText. There are more stimulating environments on the Mac, but this one is useful. And it is free.	

Application windows also retain similarities to the Desktop.

Type yourself a message. Notice that the cursor arrow changes once it's on the screen. It is now an 'I-beam'. This marks what is called the insertion point – where what you type will start. You can delete mistakes by selecting the errant text, dragging the held-down mouse over it to highlight it, and then typing over it. You could also highlight and use the delete key on the keyboard.

	Untitled	
Stimulating environments on the Mac.		
Welcome to TeachText. This one is useful. And it is free.		

Highlighting text is the the same for any Mac application.

If you want to move, rather than delete, a block of text you can highlight it, with your mouse, then pull down the edit menu and select Cut. The selected text will disappear. Place your I-beam where you want the text to start from by clicking once. Go to the Edit menu again and select Paste. Done! You have just cut and pasted, an important Macintosh activity. (For much more about working with text see Chapter 6.)

 Keep Pasting and you'll find the same piece of text you selected will keep arriving on your page. You'll also find the Scroll Bars on the right of the window will activate as the text gets longer (normally as soon as you have filled more than the window area with data). Drag the squares in the scroll bar up and down to navigate through your text – or click on the up and down arrows at the top and bottom right of the window.

Finally, if you get stuck, you can use Balloon Help. This is an Apple utility that provides a brief description of whatever part of the screen you point the cursor at. Click and hold down the question mark icon and choose Show Balloons to turn it on. When it drives you mad, or you don't need it any more, choose Hide Balloons from the same question mark menu.

Balloon help, a wonder at first, then it's a real pain in the butt.

SAVE IT

Working with most applications doesn't get much more complicated than this but there is one more essential. Once you're happy with what you've written, the work needs to be saved.

The 'Save' and 'Save As...' boxes on the Mac are consistent across almost all applications with only minor differences: you may be given different file formats to save to, or you might be allowed to create special folders as you save in some applications. The key is this:

To 'Save' means to copy the work held in the Mac's elctronic brain (its RAM). That is to say, the data that is buzzing around the Mac as long as there's electricity running through it to make it buz z, is stored safely and permanently on a magnetic medium, whether that's your hard disk or a floppy disk.

If you're working on a file that exists already – effectively you are editing it – then, when you Save, the changes you've made will become permanent.

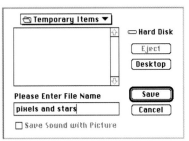

What happens if you want to save your original work and the version with changes; or if you want to save a copy of your work into a different place – a floppy,

Save and Save again, it's all your work.

for example – from within the application? You can use 'Save As…'. The command is under the File menu in

most applications. Save As means you rename your edited document under a different name, leaving your original intact. Always change the name of your document when you Save As (for example add a 'version 2', or 'final copy' to explain the difference). That way things won't get confusing. This screen shot shows work being Saved As. Using this function, you can save different

stages of edited work simply and easily.

If there's a 'File Type' option in your save box, leave it on normal – this will be the automatic setting – unless you have a reason to change it. In our example we are using *Word*, a word processor that enables you to save files in many different file formats. The reason for this is so that they can be understood by different programs –

useful for exporting information to colleagues who use different types of computer or different Macintosh applications to the ones you use.

Several file formats are open to you.

SAVE TO WHERE

Whether you want to Save for the first time, or Save As, the Save dialog is one of the most confusing dialog boxes on the Mac because it isn't at all clear how you make sure your work lands in the right place. If you hit Save on most Macs when you're working on a document that has already been stored, your document will be left exactly where it is. Save As…, though, is different.

Here's a new document ready to Save to the right place.

When Save is clicked, a dialog box appears. Choose a name for your document and

type it in but don't click the Save button, the one highlighted, yet. You'll see a box above with a list of files inside it, and above that a label.

Click on this label and you'll see a kind of route map of your Mac's entire folder structure – in this case a new file called 'Message to Karl' is in danger of landing up within a folder called 'Wild Disco arrangements', nested inside four other folders on the hard disk.

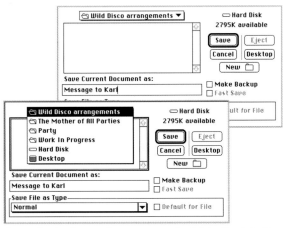

Remember to choose where you save, don't take the default.

You don't want it stored there. However, clicking any one of several options means it's possible to cycle back up through different locations towards the Desktop. Here the hard disk has been selected. You can also get there straightaway, either dragging the mouse down to the desktop or hard disk and selecting – or by clicking on Desktop to the right (this option is only available on some applications).

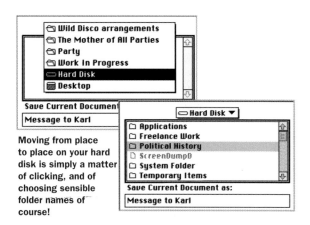

Moving from place to place on your hard disk is simply a matter of clicking, and of choosing sensible folder names of course!

Clicking on it will show all the different folders. Political History seems an appropriate folder, here.

You don't have to save a document on to the volume it was created on. You can select different storage areas – for example, on to a floppy rather than a hard disk. Here the floppy is labelled 'ixels'.

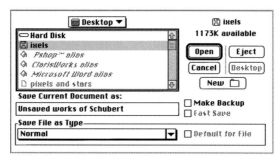

Saving straight to floppy disk couldn't be any simpler.

Notice in this dialog box from a Microsoft *Word 5.0* document there is also an option to create a whole new folder. This is useful if you're starting a new project and you haven't set up a specific folder for it.

Once you've saved your document, the dialog box won't reappear every time you pick Save from the File menu. Changes will simply be added – you know this is being done because you'll see the cursor turn into the Mac clock while it's happening.

The problem with the Save As… option is that, unless you tell it otherwise, it will send your document to the last folder you selected when you used the Save command for your document. If you were saving because you wanted to keep the new document back-up separate from the original, this can be a pain. However, a

little patience and some proper navigation, and you should be able to make good use of the two Save options.

On Performas, files saved using Save As will always be sent to the Document folder on the hard disk unless you say otherwise. (You can use the Find commands in the desktop to retrieve errant files; see Chapter 2).

CLOSING UP

Closing a document is different from Quitting the application. Closing is like turning a new leaf in a colouring book. Quitting is closing the colouring book, washing the paintbrush, and making a coffee. If you really have finished it's a good idea to quit the program. Macs can do two or three things at once, but they can do them faster with more memory freed up. Quitting means you're actually closing down the application, rather than closing a document. 'Quit' and 'Close' are two separate commands in the File menu of all applications.

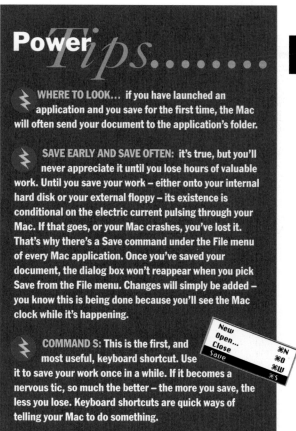

Power *Tips.........*

WHERE TO LOOK… if you have launched an application and you save for the first time, the Mac will often send your document to the application's folder.

SAVE EARLY AND SAVE OFTEN: it's true, but you'll never appreciate it until you lose hours of valuable work. Until you save your work – either onto your internal hard disk or your external floppy – its existence is conditional on the electric current pulsing through your Mac. If that goes, or your Mac crashes, you've lost it. That's why there's a Save command under the File menu of every Mac application. Once you've saved your document, the dialog box won't reappear when you pick Save from the File menu. Changes will simply be added – you know this is being done because you'll see the Mac clock while it's happening.

COMMAND S: This is the first, and most useful, keyboard shortcut. Use it to save your work once in a while. If it becomes a nervous tic, so much the better – the more you save, the less you lose. Keyboard shortcuts are quick ways of telling your Mac to do something.

PRINT WORKS

Paper is not redundant. You need to print…

There are two steps to printing on the Mac. One is setting up your printer – you do this once. The other is printing. Presumably you intend to do this often, and you've obviously invested in a printer…

THE FIRST STEPS TO PRINTING

Make sure you loaded the software that came with your printer. Make sure the printer is connected to either the printer or the modem port, or via the SCSI port, if that's what the manual tells you to do.

Open the Chooser under the Apple Menu (the Apple logo at the left-hand side of your screen). Click-hold and select Chooser to reach it.

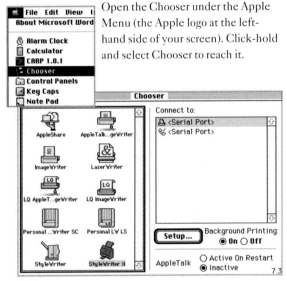

Setting up your printer is a piece of cake with the Chooser.

You'll find a thumbnail picture of your printer on the left-hand side of the screen. Selecting this will bring up the name of the printer, or an option for which port you're using, on the right-hand side. Select it. You can now close the box – there's no 'Confirm' button.

Don't worry about the AppleTalk reference unless you're connected to a PostScript printer – in which case check it on. (If you want more detailed information on the Chooser, turn to Chapter 4.)

There's also an option called Background Printing. If you check this box, your printer will print while you carry on working in other applications. A 'System Extension' called Print Monitor, which will have been installed automatically on your system, controls background printing. It launches as you hit Print, and

can be called up from the Finder icon-menu at the far right of the menu bar – but only when you are actually printing. (For more information on background printing, see Chapter 4).

Those are the options. Once you close the Chooser, your Mac should find the printer. Back to the business of printing a document. Pull down the File menu and select Print. Alternatively use a keyboard shortcut: the keyboard command for print is Command P. (Hit the command key on your keyboard – it's the one with the Apple on it – and hit P at the same time). Either method brings up a print dialog box. This varies slightly from printer to printer and application to application but basically enables the number of copies and the number of pages – including a specific range of pages – to be set, ready for printing at varying qualities – Draft, Normal or Best in this case, using black and white or greyscale.

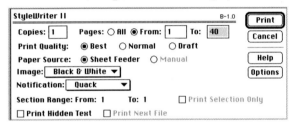

With even the lowest-cost printer there's a range of options.

The example shows a StyleWriter II – one of the less expensive Apple-made printers – it's ideal for use with

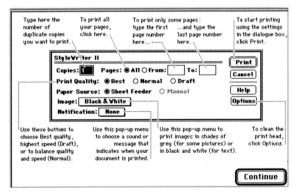

home machines. Here's a handy tip for people with StyleWriters: Pressing the Help button on the StyleWriter dialog box gives you all the help you'll need explaining each option.

At heart though, printing from a Mac, no matter what kind of printer you are using should be a piece of cake. Normally, once you've got your printer set up, all you have to do is press Command and P and you're away.

WHAT ABOUT POSTSCRIPT?

There is only one other point you need to know about printing with your Mac, and that's about the printing 'languages'. There are two kinds of printers – PostScript printers and QuickDraw printers. QuickDraw is the Mac's own language, used to display what you see on screen. QuickDraw printers use this information when they print, so will print exactly what you see. StyleWriters, for example, are QuickDraw printers.

Apple is in the throes of developing a new version of QuickDraw called QuickDraw GX which should provide QuickDraw printers using TrueType fonts with the ability to produce higher quality work.

PostScript printers use a Page Description Language called PostScript to turn mathematically derived outlines into dots that the printer outputs. The Apple 600 series printers are PostScript printers as, in fact, are high quality imagesetters used by commercial reprographic bureaus.

Choosing a printer depends on what you want to do with it. With graphics-heavy work you will really need a PostScript printer – and if you're going to take work to bureaus you'll also find that life will be simpler if you use Postscript.

If you're not, then using a QuickDraw printer and TrueType fonts (see below), a small set of which come ready-installed with the Mac, may well be fine.

WHICH FONTS

It's worth knowing something about fonts and typefaces because one of the best parts of having a Mac is that you can make everything from laundry lists up look dauntingly beautiful. This will be useful if you become famous (or are famous), write a novel or whatever. Or want to impress the local laundromat.

There are around 6,000 digitized fonts that work with a Mac. The vast majority of these will either be PostScript (also called Type 1) fonts, or TrueType fonts. TrueType is a font system developed by Microsoft and Apple, which does not use PostScript. Both these fonts are scalable; that is, they can generate fonts for any size of a particular typeface, on screen and in print. There are some City fonts: Geneva and Chicago for example, that only exist as screen fonts and that cannot be scaled. These have to be loaded in specific sizes. These are bitmap fonts. (To make everything more complicated,

Power *Tips*...........

A WORD ABOUT BUTTONS Buttons look like this. They provide options to click. You'll notice that in most dialog boxes they'll either be faded out, black or black with heavily lined edges. If they're faded, you can't access them (there can be different reasons for this). If they're outlined with a thin line they're available options and you can select them by clicking. If they're outlined with a heavy line, they're the default option – the action the Mac thinks you're going to want to take.

Hitting Return on the keyboard will activate pre-selected, that is heavily outlined, options, saving the bother of mousing up to the dialog box, and double clicking.

TO DEINSTALL A FONT, first Quit everything. Your Mac won't let you move the font files out of the System folder until you do.

SPEEDIER WORKING, can be obtained without adding anything special to your Mac if you remember one thing: you don't have to work in anything more than black and white.

For example, if you are doing word processing work, tidying your Mac, creating a basic spreadsheet or database or getting online with a communications package, you can work in black and white. in fact not using thousands of hues or shades of black and white can speed up data entry and window re-draws quite dramatically. A neat shortcut to switch between colour and black and white is to make an alias of the Monitor control panel (you will find this in the Control Panel folder within the System Folder).

Once you have made the alias you can then store it in the Apple Menu Items folder (more about this in Chapter 4) or on the Desktop. Double-clicking on this alias will bring up the Monitor control panel. Now all you need to do is to click on the black and white option when you want to carry out simple tasks, and then click back on the shades you require when you need to do heavy work.

some bitmap fonts have TrueType, scalable, versions.)

Books have been written about the merits and demerits of each system. The most salient point for now is don't mix up the two standards. Your Mac comes shipped with TrueType fonts; don't install PostScript fonts of the same name without deinstalling your TrueType ones first. It will confuse your printer (and you) then you won't produce a good result.

That's it then… you're up and running, producing, printing and you know how to Quit. Your Macintosh is your Oyster. Next Stop – The Finder…

✚ DON'T PANIC

If you spill coffee, tea, red wine or worse into your keyboard you must power down and disconnect it immediately. Don't re-connect until dry or you could short-circuit your entire machine. To clean your keyboard turn it upside down and use a slightly damp cloth. If you spill anything sticky or sugary on your keyboard, get help from your dealer.

Below you can see a range of fonts. Font size is measured in 'points', abbreviated 'pt'. The effects below were obtained by altering standard faces that come with most Macintoshes in a word processing program.

This is Times 36 pt

This is Times 36 pt bold

This is Monaco at 36pt too

This is Monaco at 36pt

This is Times at 24pt

This is Times at 24pt

This is Monaco at 24pt too

This is Monaco at 24pt too

This is Times 12 pt

This is Times 12 pt

This is Monaco at 12pt too

THIS IS MONACO AT 12PT TOO

Finders Keepers

The door to all your work

The Finder

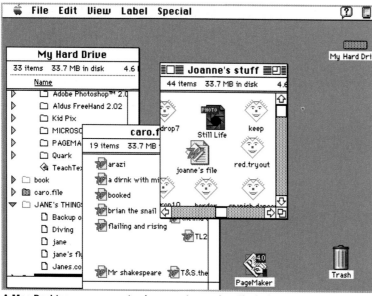

2

A Mac Desktop: you can customize yours to your heart's desire.

You've got the Mac... you've got some software... now you need to organize yourself. This is where the Desktop and its companion, the Finder, come to the rescue. The Mac's Finder software is the finest pieces of computer operating system design ever to be presented to a human being. It enables you to copy, delete, move, keep track of, and generally stay in control of all the files you will find on your Mac. The Desktop is its place of work. This chapter will tell you about shortcuts, tricks and even some of the basics that will put you in control of both...

You may think it's OK to plug in some cables, power up, hit Microsoft *Word* and write your bestseller: and with a Mac you can do just that. However, while it's fine to be minimalist about computing, it's useful to know enough about your Mac to make it work for you rather than against you.

At some point you'll realize it would be nice to know how to sort out your back-up files, your character lists, your edited versions; it would be nice to know how to get your Mac to start specific applications when it starts up. It would even be nice to know that you can stop it beeping like a mad thing, or turn on Sticky Keys if you've broken your wrist and you can't use keyboard shortcuts because you can't hold two keys down at once. The Finder can do all these things for you.

Here is a caveat for Performa owners: the Performa Desktop isn't exactly like the standard Mac Desktop. That's because it includes a special piece of software called 'Launcher'. You may want to run the Performa with the Launcher but for most users a better idea is to disable it and run the Mac like a 'proper' Mac. This may take slightly longer to learn but it is more flexible. To find out more, turn to the specific Performa section later in this chapter.

The standard Mac Desktop functions something like the physical kind and, like a physical desktop, it can get gummed up. The big difference is that with the Mac you can file as you create.

The Desktop is made up very simply. On the far left at the top is the Apple menu, which you can also see in all applications. The Apple icon is part of a Menu bar along the top of the screen. There are different options under each pull-down menu – click with the mouse and the options will appear. To the right-hand end of this bar there's the Balloon Help query button. To the right of that is the Finder or application icon.

On the ideal Desktop (and there's no reason to arrange yours this way although it may be simplest if more than one person is using the machine) the hard disk is to the top right of the screen and the Wastebasket is at the bottom right.

There can also be icons representing any floppies, CD-ROM drives or additional hard disks that are 'mounted' (connected) to your Mac. The screenshot above shows that the hard disk is open and so is darkened. You may also have windows showing the contents of open disks. These windows can display their contents as icons, small icons, or as lists of text.

Finders Keepers

HIERARCHIES

▦	My Hard Drive		▭▯
3 items	33.8 MB in disk		4.6 MB available

Name		Size	Kind
▷ ☐ Applications		–	folder
▷ ☐ System Folder		–	folder
▷ ☐ Work In Progress		–	folder

A simple window showing the contents of a hard disk.

The Mac uses a hierarchical filing system that works via a series of folders that can be examined through windows. Here the hard disk: 'My Hard Drive' has been opened to reveal a series of folders: 'System Folder', 'Work in Progress' folder and an 'Applications' folder. We're looking at it as a series of Names. Any of the folders can be opened to show further levels of organization. If your desktop doesn't look like this, and you want it to, go to the View menu and choose 'by Name'.

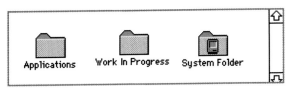

Navigating around your Mac is simply a case of remembering the hierarchy of Disk>Folder>File-or-document. You can either view these in text or pictorial (icon) format.

Within each folder may be more folders – nested in a hierarchical way. Double clicking on the folder view gives a route map of the nesting process. Different views of the

files provide different means of sorting them. Obviously there's a compromise between order and overdoing the folder>sub-folder>sub-folder>file-or-document route. Below left, the route from a file in a folder we have set up called 'Bribes Offered' is via five other folders. Fortunately though, Mac windows are aware of their roots – as you'll see when we come to copying and moving files.

To make a new folder, click in the window of the disk or folder in which you want your folder to be located. For example if your folder is for letters about your overdraft, click inside your 'Letters to Bank Manager' folder; then go to the File menu and choose New Folder – it will appear as 'untitled'. Type in a name, 'Answered Mail' for example, and you have a new folder.

A WORD ABOUT WINDOWS

▯▭	Party		▭▯
8 items	34 MB in disk		4.4 MB av

Handily, the top (title) bar is same for hard or floppy disks.

To move a window around the screen, click on the title bar – anywhere but in the square corner boxes at either end – and drag it to where you want to go. To resize a window, grab the lower right-hand corner with the mouse and pull out. To close a window, click the square in the top left corner, or mouse all the way up to the File menu option where there's a Close Window option. The quick to do this is to use the keyboard shortcut: Command W. To do this press the command key and W at the same time. Document windows within applications behave in almost exactly the same way as these ones on the Desktop.

You'll notice that only one window is active at once – and this window will come to the front as you click on it. In our screen shot the 'Party Budget' window is active despite the fact that you can't actually see the file.

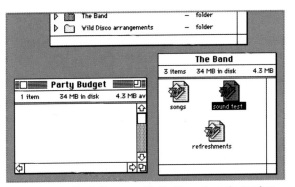

The active window is the one with the lines along the top bar.

MOVING FILES

In the Finder, you can move files from place to place by dragging them from one window to another – or from one folder to another within a window. Select the file, keep the mouse key down, and drag. As long as the location you're moving the file to is on the same physical volume – the same hard disk, for example – this will move the file. If you move a file from a hard disk to a floppy, the file will be copied onto the floppy – leaving you an unasked for but often in retrospect, appreciated, back-up file.

financially risky projects		
0 items	34.1 MB in	
Name		

Sure Fire Winners			
1 item	34.1 MB in disk	4.2 MB availa	
Name		Size	Kind
▷ 📁 MY LIFE'S WORK		–	

financially risky projects		
1 item	34.1 MB in	
Name		
▷ 📁 MY LIFE'S WORK		

Sure Fire Winners			
0 items	34.1 MB in disk	4.3 MB availa	
Name		Size	Kind

Moving files from folder to folder with a mouse is easy.

Suppose you want to drag loads of files to a new location. This is very simple. If the files you want are in a folder, you can move the whole folder. In the shots above, the folder 'My Life's Work' has been moved from the 'Sure Fire Winners' to the Folder 'Financially Risky Projects'.

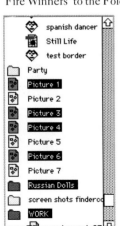

If the files you want are scattered around a window or windows, that's fine too – you can handle it using a process called Shift-Select. Choose a file, select it, keep the shift key down and keep on selecting. Whatever you click on will be selected and can be moved (or deleted) as one. You can select files and folders or a combination of the two.

Select more than one item at a time by pressing Shift and then selecting.

You can also Drag-Select around a whole group of files. Click once on a blank area of the screen, drag out a square, and release the mouse. Anything in the square will be selected. Drag your highlighted files to their new location by clicking on one of them, holding the mouse-button down and pulling. Where the cursor points the files will land.

If you want to rename a file or a folder or a disk, highlight the title bar, wait for the pointer arrow to turn into an I-beam and then type in the new name.

VIEWING THE DESKTOP

If you've put a file in a folder, that's where it stays. You can see this arrangement in a number of ways by selecting different views: small icon, icon or name from the View menu. Icon views enables you to organize related files in groups visually, so you might group files about work to the left, files about holidays to the right. You can clean up files in a particular window using the Clean Up Desktop command under the Special menu.

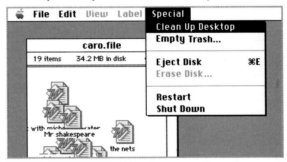

You can even tidy up your work area with a menu option.

Using the Views control panel (see later), you can set windows to show three useful pieces of information – the number of items in the folder you are viewing; the amount of data stored on the hard or floppy disk; the amount of free space. This is useful if you want to keep track of the state of your hard or floppy disk – a full disk is no use.

🍎 File Edit View Label Special				? 📋
The Mother of All Parties				
4 items		34.3 MB in disk		4 MB available
Name	Size	Kind	Label	Last Modified
▷ 📁 lighting	–	folder	–	Sun, Sep 5, 1993, 6:
▷ 📁 Party Budget	–	folder	–	Sun, Sep 5, 1993, 6:
▷ 📁 The Band	–	folder	–	Sun, Sep 5, 1993, 6:
▷ 📁 Wild Disco arrangements	–	folder	–	Sun, Sep 5, 1993, 6:

Find out what's on your disks with one glance at a window.

Finders Keepers

View | **Label** | **S**
by Small Icon
by Icon
✓ by Name
by Size
by Kind
by Label
by Date

Organizing files by name has the advantage that you can see how files are nested. Clicking the triangular indicators expands and closes folder lists.

Using Name, you get more details about your files – including name, label, and the date it was last modified. The Name view is just one choice in the View menu, and you don't need to use this to change a view in an open window. Simply select the view you want by clicking the list headings. Below, Name is selected, and then Size – so the order of the files has changed to reflect these priorities.

JANE's Projects

5 items		34.4 MB in disk		3.9 MB available
Name	Size	Kind	Label	Last Modified
🗋 Backup of Diving	74K	Microsoft Word do...	–	Thu, Aug 26, 1
🗋 Diving	39K	Microsoft Word do...	–	Fri, Aug 13, 19
🗋 Jane's fly sheet	27K	PageMaker document	–	Fri, Jun 18, 19
🗋 Janes.conf.doc	20K	PageMaker document	–	Mon, Jan 4, 19
🗋 Jane	11K	Microsoft Word do...	–	Tue, May 11, 1

JANE's Projects

5 items		34.4 MB in disk		4 MB available
Name	Size	Kind	Label	Last Modified
🗋 Backup of Diving	74K	Microsoft Word do...	–	Thu, Aug 26, 1
🗋 Diving	39K	Microsoft Word do...	–	Fri, Aug 13, 19
🗋 Jane	11K	Microsoft Word do...	–	Tue, May 11, 1
🗋 Jane's fly sheet	27K	PageMaker document	–	Fri, Jun 18, 19
🗋 Janes.conf.doc	20K	PageMaker document	–	Mon, Jan 4, 19

View your folders in a number of ways for ease of access.

Another way of viewing, and organizing, files is with Labels. Colour coding is easy to sneer at but it works. You'll need to use the Label menu that enables you to apply different colours either to single files or groups of files. Later you can search and sort using these categories. Here I've given labels to the following files: 'The Band' is a hot priority, while 'Party Budget' is cool. The default

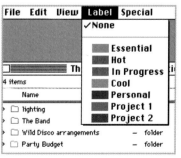

File Edit View **Label** Special
✓ None
Essential
Hot
In Progress
Cool
Personal
Project 1
Project 2

Th
4 items
Name
▶ 🗋 lighting
▶ 🗋 The Band
▶ 🗋 Wild Disco arrangements   – folder
▶ 🗋 Party Budget   – folder

criteria for different labels can be changed using the Labels control panel (see Chapter 3) if you prefer to personalize your priorities. Otherwise just use them as they are.

Now that you understand Windows and Files and how to throw them away, here are some other useful tools under the File menu option.

THE GET INFO COMMAND

One other way of adding or getting information about any file, folder or application is the Get Info command. Select a file and then use Get Info under the File menu or use Command I from the keyboard. This provides a list of useful information, including file-size and kind (for example *Kid Pix* as in the shot below), where created (you get a precise location) and when your folder was modified. Get Info enables you to tag comments onto your work. You can also lock a document from here (it can be Saved As…, or copied but once locked the original is safe).

Get Info boxes look slightly different depending on the kind of item (folder, file, application, System Extension, aliase) you've opened. Applications boxes, for example, give you options to change the amount of memory you've allocated to the application.

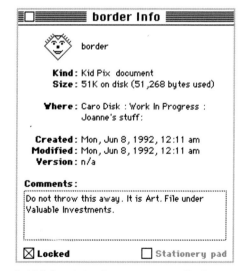

border Info

border

Kind: Kid Pix document
Size: 51K on disk (51,268 bytes used)

Where: Caro Disk : Work In Progress :
Joanne's stuff:

Created: Mon, Jun 8, 1992, 12:11 am
Modified: Mon, Jun 8, 1992, 12:11 am
Version: n/a

Comments:
Do not throw this away. It is Art. File under
Valuable Investments.

☒ **Locked**   ☐ Stationery pad

Get Info is only two key-presses away. Use it.

ALIASES SAVE TIME AND SPACE

The Alias system from Apple is aimed at helping you store and group your work in a way that suits you while retaining direct access to folders, files or applications. Aliases are not files but pointers to files, and you can put them anywhere on your Mac. They give you direct, one-click access to your work. They take up very little space

– around 1-2K (that's practically nothing) – so you can have as many aliases are you like.

Say for example that you want to keep all your applications in one place; they're valuable and you don't want to mix them up with your documents. However, you have a project that involves using two applications – say *MacWrite* and *Intellidraw*. There's also a series of documents you've got stored in different places on your Mac. If you make aliases of all of these, and put them in a folder – or even on the Desktop – you can find everything you need without searching every folder on your Mac.

A second example: you use *Word* all the time – so leave an alias on the desktop. A third: you've lent your machine to a graphic artist friend who has promised to jazz up some documents for you – leave her a single folder with aliases of the relevant applications and the files she'll need.

You can have as many aliases of a single file as you like – just keep making them. Basically, aliases leave your Mac to do all the finding.

To make an alias go to the Make Alias command under the File menu. Notice that you can make aliases of an alias – although you'd be better off making aliases of the original.

Aliases of aliases: like circles within circles, except useful.

Having made aliases you need to leave them in places where they provide a one-stop locator for files when they are needed. Think of this as putting TV remote controls at useful points around your TV room. The default name for an alias, by the way, is *filename alias* (aliases are created in italic). So the alias of a file called Job would be *Job alias*, simple but effective.

You can change the name of an alias and it will still find its original file. This is useful if you want immediate access to a file but you don't particularly want it to advertise its contents. Here a cunningly renamed 'Very Productive Work' alias, left out on the Desktop for instant access, is actually the path to a new CV. ... as you can see when Get

Info is used. This gives the 'route' of the original when prompted by hitting the Find Original button.

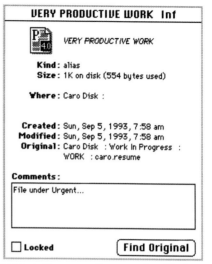

Get Info to the rescue, it even works with aliases.

One other point about aliases. If your Mac is networked to other people, you can access files held on a server (a central computer) simply by creating an an alias of it (ask your System Manager if you're not sure about your particular network). Once you have managed to access a file on another machine, you can make an alias of that too. Select it in the usual way, select Make Alias from the File menu and drag the alias to your Desktop.

25

LOST & FOUND

Enough about Desktop file management. What happens when it breaks down? Either you were in a hurry and called your file something uninformative like 'Dubious Stuff', or you called it something sensible but not distinctive enough – you have a million files called 'Flight of the bumble bee' because that's your PhD subject. Or you did put it in the right place, but it's just not there (that

is, you didn't put it in the right place…). A hint: if you take files from other people, change the names so they make sense to you.

If you lose a file, help is a click away via the reasonably wonderful Find and Find Again commands under the File menu.(Command F is the shortcut) Depending how you left it last time you'll get one of two boxes:

Finders Keepers

The Find box is very straightforward. Type in the name, or part of the name, of the file you want to find – Find doesn't differentiate between lower and upper case. Your Mac will find the first file that meets the criteria you've set.

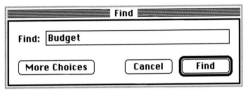

You don't have to lose track of files with Command F.

If you want to search for more files use the Find Again command under the File menu bar (the keyboard shortcut is Command G). You can keep pressing Command G until you've found all the instances of files by a particular name.

This won't help you of course, if you've misnamed your file but you can define more choices. Choose Find and hit the More Choices button – this enables you to search by different categories. Note that one option is to search by Comment – these are the comments you can affix using the Get Info box.

Other ways of setting the parameters of your search, change depending on which primary search category (name or date, for example) you've chosen. If you select date, you can ask for a search on a specific date or you can ask for before or after options. To change the date backwards or forwards click on it.

You can also set boundaries to your search (search all mounted disks, just a floppy, just your hard disk…) using the Search button. It's also possible to search Selected Items, say two or three folders, as the shot below shows. The check box All At Once enables you either to bring up items one at a time or all together – in the latter case you'll see them highlighted in a list view (even if you generally use icon views) with a useful note saying how many there are. You may not see them all if you run out of window space, if that is so you'll need to scroll down.

Try search by date too see how much work you've done today.

The flexibility of the Find function means it can be used to do more than locate lost files. If you use it wisely, it can be used to organize back ups, lock and unlock files, to regroup applications, to find files labelled by type, or to housekeep your hard disk. You can throw away – or archive – large files that are clogging up your disk that you don't need, if you sort by size. Perhaps you've finished a job and want to archive all the files concerned with it – use Find to select and then you can move them.

TRASHING FILES

Trashing files, folders and applications is very simple. Drag them to the Wastebasket, which will swell up to indicate that it has items in it. This doesn't mean that you've actually erased the items though. All you've done is discarded them. They stay in your Wastebasket until you go to the Special menu and select Empty Wastebasket. At this point you'll get an alert dialog explaining you are about to do an irrevocable thing.

Make sure you want to trash items.

Remember that your Mac will apply any command you choose to give it to whatever you've selected. If you delete a folder, all the contents will be binned alongside the folder.

If you want to kill a folder but not the contents, empty it first by moving the contents elsewhere.

If you want to see what's in the Wastebasket – double click it. If you change your mind about binning something, drag it back out onto the hard disk.

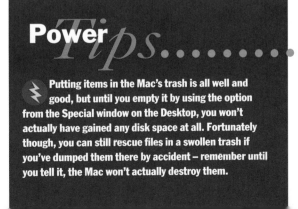

Power *Tips*

Putting items in the Mac's trash is all well and good, but until you empty it by using the option from the Special window on the Desktop, you won't actually have gained any disk space at all. Fortunately though, you can still rescue files in a swollen trash if you've dumped them there by accident – remember until you tell it, the Mac won't actually destroy them.

MOVING ITEMS AROUND

You can now move, sort and copy/duplicate. Here's how…

Dragging files around *within* a volume – that's within a hard disk, or within a floppy – *moves* them. Dragging them *between* volumes – between a hard disk and a floppy disk, for example – *copies* them.

Below we have used a screenshot of a file called 'Moveable Feasts' on a floppy disk. If we select the file (Moveable Feasts) and drag it to the folder called 'Party Budgets' on the hard disk – it will be copied.

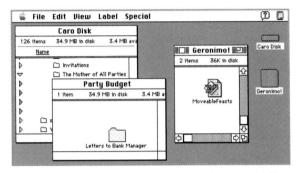

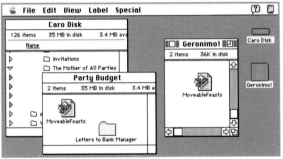

Once again, manipulating files is a simple mousing action.

Try it the other way and it won't work – 'Party Budgets' is too large to fit on the floppy disk (called 'Geronimo'). Helpfully, the Mac will warn that space is short so that you can try a new disk or maybe try to free some space .

Your Mac will make sure that you don't waste your time.

If you want to copy a file or folder within a volume – perhaps you want to edit one version and keep an original – use the Duplicate command under the File menu. You can duplicate single files, folders and their contents or several folders at once (use Shift-select and then Command D to do this).

The slow method uses menus. Press Command D for speed.

If you want to copy the entire contents of a floppy disk onto your hard drive highlight the floppy disk and drag the icon over the hard disk – then let go. The files will automatically be copied and will be placed in a folder on your disk. It works backwards too – if you want to copy a folder onto a floppy select it and drag it unopened across to the floppy icon. Release it, and you're away.

WORKING WITH FLOPPY DISKS

We've already explained how to copy items onto a floppy disk and from a floppy to a hard disk. You may also want to erase floppy disks. Erasing completely expunges files. It also makes disks ready to use – in fact, erasing is actually the same process as initializing (see below). Think of it as sweeping a gravel pathway smooth.

To erase a floppy disk you'll need to go to the Special menu, pull down the menu and select Erase Disk. Confirm at the warning window (assuming the disk is the disk you want to erase and not, for example, the entire contents of a hard disk – it's wise to check). Once your disk is erased it will sit quietly on the desktop waiting to be ejected or renamed.

Make sure that you really want to lose all the data on that disk.

Finders Keepers

INITIALIZING A FLOPPY DISK

If a disk can't be recognized you'll need to initialize it before you can use it. Beware! This means erasing anything that was on the disk previously. And erasing is permanent. There is one warning here: if you want to get data from a disk that was created by another kind of computer, your Mac will ask if you want it initialized. If you want to keep the data, you musn't say yes – the disk should be ejected instead.

To initialize, follow the on-screen instructions and choose 'Two-sided' if this option is given (some old disks cannot be initialized this way). If you want to abort your mission, choose Eject. At the end of the initializing you'll be prompted for a name. All new floppy disks need initializing before they will work.

You can eject a disk using the command under the Special menu on the Desktop – or you can use the keyboard shortcut of Command E on the keyboard. (If you have problems – for example, if your disk won't eject – see Troubleshooting in Chapter 13.)

HOW TO EDIT

One menu option on the Finder we haven't looked at so far is the Edit menu. This includes a set of basic commands you'll already have found are consistent right the way through the Mac. They are Cut, Copy and Paste. You don't actually use them much in the Finder; they come into their own for cutting and pasting text, graphics and sounds within and across documents. You definitely need to know about these commands to get going.

Cutting text (or graphics) means selecting and *removing* material from a document, or even a file name, into a central store called the Clipboard.

Copying text (or graphics) means selecting and *copying* material from a document into a central store, once again the Clipboard.

Until you've cut and copied material to place on your Clipboard, the Paste option will be faded out – you obviously can't paste if there's nothing there.

Pasting text (or graphics) means placing a copy of what is on the Clipboard into any viable location you have selected. To Paste put the cursor where you want to insert your cut or copied material and choose Paste from

the Edit menu. Alternatively, press Command and then V for the keyboard shortcut.

If you select Show Clipboard from the Edit menu, you can see what's been loaded ready to paste.

In the context of the Finder you could use cutting and pasting with the Get Info box. For example, you could copy and paste information from one file to a related later file. If you're not happy with this concept, practice it. (See Chapter 6 for more details on cutting and pasting.)

HOW TO UNDO

Undo is one of the most useful commands ever. You'll find it under Edit in the Finder, and it is also a feature of most applications you will use on your Mac. Undo will literally undo your last action. To Undo, you must not do anything between the action you want to undo and using the Undo command. The basic rule is that if you make a mistake, you should press Undo **IMMEDIATELY**.

Undo works by remembering what you did last; this is why you shouldn't do anything else in between. So, for example, if you are word processing and you delete a whole section of a document, go to Undo. The Mac will look at the last command (Delete) and undo it. If, in the meantime, you scroll up the document to see the damage, and correct a spelling mistake, Undo will undo the correction, not the original mistake. Some applications, particularly graphics ones, however, do have a number of levels of undo (say, the last four or five commands). **Undo first, ask questions later.**

BALLOONS AND THE FINDER ICON

More advanced Mac users should never forget the power of the beginner's best friend: Balloon Help. This little gem is used to get context-specific help. You will find it at the top right of the Desktop screen, just next to the Finder icon. As well as being able to switch it on and find out about your Mac,

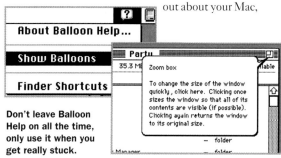

Don't leave Balloon Help on all the time, only use it when you get really stuck.

more and more applications (word processors, paint packages…) are making use of Balloon Help. A hint: only switch on Balloon Help when you are really lost. If you have it on all the time, it will slow you down horribly.

Next to Balloon Help is the Finder icon (see the screenshot above). This is actually a brilliant way to navigate. Within applications you'll see the application icon at the top of the window; drag down that and you'll find the Finder icon; click on the Finder and you're back where you started from. The screenshot shows the Mac flicking from *Word* to the Finder. Of course, you can also move from application to application or even from an application to the Desktop with ease.

If things are getting confusing – when there are many programs open at once, for example – this icon can be used to hide everything you don't want to see, but you do want to leave running. You will use the Finder icon more and more to save you time and effort.

PRINTING

Printing from the Desktop is simple. Select the file you want to print, go to Print in the File menu and you're away. Your Mac will then launch the application, launch the print dialogue box – you need to click OK on the parameters – and then print. If you want to batch print (that is, print many files at once) you can select the files you want to print by Shift-selecting, then hit Print as before. The first file to be printed will give you a dialog box; after that the printer will either simply keep going in the best cases, or ask you to confirm each time a new document is launched (this depends on the application used to create the documents).

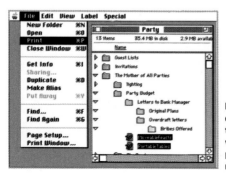

Print files directly from the Desktop with a simple pull-down menu system.

DATA SECURITY

Once you've created your work, you will need to look after it. In some cases you will even need to protect it from accidental deletion. One excellent way of doing this is to 'lock' it. To achieve this on a file for example, select it with the mouse then use Command I or Get Info under the File menu to bring up the Get Info box. Check the lock file box, so that it has an X in it. Locked files can be

opened and Saved As… but they cannot be changed in themselves. This is useful if you need to protect the integrity of the document and also need to use it as a template or a reference. You can lock files on floppies too but it may be better to protect the entire disk.

Opening the small tab in the right-hand corner of the disk so that you can see through it, locks it. You can display the contents of a locked disk (but a small padlock appears in the top of the window to indicate that you can't copy to or from it). You can open locked items, you copy them but you can't change the originals.

There is one other essential method of securing your data: Back it up – make regular copies of all your important data and keep the copies (which you've probably saved to floppy disks) away from your Mac; for example, if your Mac is at work, keep the copies at home and vice versa.

Power *Tips* . . . .

LOCKED FILES: you can throw locked files away but only on purpose. To do so, drag the chosen file to the Mac's trash, hold down the Option key while choosing the Empty command from the Special menu, and the files will disappear… forever.

FINDING SHORTCUT HELP: there's a Finder Shortcuts option under Balloon Help. It provides an on-line list of useful keyboard shortcuts to make moving around faster, easier. Print it out, learn them, and you'll know more than most users do.

THE SYSTEM FOLDER

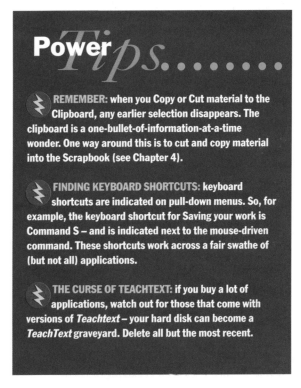

System Folder

19 items   35.2 MB in disk   3.1 MB available

Startup Items   Audio CD Access   Apple Menu Items   Clipboard   Extensions   Control Panels

Finder   Preferences   Scrapbook File   System   MoviePlayer™   Note Pad File

There are a host of goodies lurking inside your System folder – don't mess around with anything until you're sure what you're up to.

The last area we ought to mention is the System Folder. This isn't quite like any other folder on your Mac. It's really the heart of the beast.

Inside a System Folder you'll see a System file; this is the powerhouse of the Mac. You'll also see drivers for printers or other devices. Although you can use the Find command on the Desktop to look for items inside the System *Folder*, you can't use it on the System *file*.

A sub-folder in the System Folder called Apple Menu Items holds items for the Apple Menu. You will also find the Scrapbook file in your System Folder – this holds images, text and sounds for the Scrapbook (find this in the Apple Menu, top left on your desktop).

When you install different applications you may find that some files from these are put into a Preferences folder in the System Folder, or in a separate folder created when you install. For example, there are preference files for *ClarisWorks* in a folder by this name in the System Folder. There is also a Startup Items Folder; applications stored in this folder will automatically launch when you start your Mac. A quicker way to get at items in the Control Panels is to go through the Apple menu. (To find out how to install a program into the Apple menu see Chapter 5.)

To install anything into the System Folder **SHUT IT FIRST**. This is because there is an Apple installed system of internal folders within the System Folder. Dragging a file onto the System icon enables the Mac to store 'extra bits' in the right place.

To throw away items from the System Folder, simply open the required folder and drag them out.

It's difficult to throw a System Folder away – you can't

if you are running the System – but it is relatively simple to end up with two system folders (if you back up your entire hard disk to an external drive, for example). Don't do this, it could give your Mac schizophrenia. If you need a System boot-disk (and it's a good idea to have one) make a copy using the install software that came with your Mac.

Power*Tips*. . . . .

REMEMBER: when you Copy or Cut material to the Clipboard, any earlier selection disappears. The clipboard is a one-bullet-of-information-at-a-time wonder. One way around this is to cut and copy material into the Scrapbook (see Chapter 4).

FINDING KEYBOARD SHORTCUTS: keyboard shortcuts are indicated on pull-down menus. So, for example, the keyboard shortcut for Saving your work is Command S – and is indicated next to the mouse-driven command. These shortcuts work across a fair swathe of (but not all) applications.

THE CURSE OF TEACHTEXT: if you buy a lot of applications, watch out for those that come with versions of *Teachtext* – your hard disk can become a *TeachText* graveyard. Delete all but the most recent.

Control Freaks

Customising your Mac using Control Panels

3

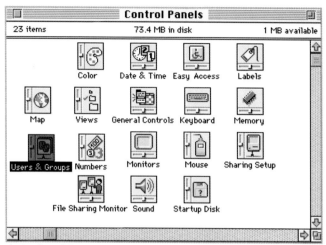

Just a few of the control panels available for the Mac.

There are control panels, consisting of simple sliders and buttons, for adapting almost every aspect of your Mac environment for your personal comfort; from changing the pattern and colour of your Mac screen to recording your own alert sounds. You can, for example, alter the type and the size of the fonts in the title bars of windows to make them easier to read. (A selection of control panels is shown on the left.) Control panels are part of the Mac's system software – the portfolio of system programs you got when you acquired your Mac. They are kept, with the rest of the Mac system software, in the System Folder. To find them, first double-click on the hard disk icon in the top right hand corner of your Mac; locate the system folder among the folders you find there and, again, double click to open it; finally, locate the control panels icon, double click again and you will find yourself at the nerve centre of your Mac. The exact line up may differ slightly from those shown in the picture.

GENERAL CONTROLS

The first thing most people do to stamp their identity on their Mac is to change the desktop pattern – the uninspiring screen background that comes with most Macs. To do this, the first thing you have to do is to double click on the General Controls control panel icon.

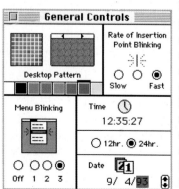

General Controls: it's just the start.

In most cases the panel will open to reveal a window similar to the one shown left. (If your Mac is a Performa, a simplified version of this screen will appear.) The top left-hand enclosure in this window shows two boxes

and a coloured ribbon (the ribbon will contain only greys if your Mac is not a colour machine, or will be absent if your Mac is a Performa). The right-hand box displays the selected pattern as it looks on the desktop. The left-hand box shows a magnified version of the current

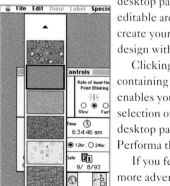

Select a design from the Performa's patterns.

desktop pattern and provides an editable area where you can create your own unique desktop design with a few clicks.

Clicking on the scroll bar containing the two tiny arrows enables you to choose from a selection of pre-programmed desktop patterns. (With a Performa this is all you can do).

If you feel like getting a little more adventurous, on most Macs you can create your own desktop pattern.

First click on one of the colours in the ribbon. Your cursor then becomes your paintbrush. To add or remove colours, click in the left-hand box. Your masterpiece appears in the miniature screen giving you a test view at the same time as you are creating it.

Once you have achieved the perfect desktop pattern, don't close the control panel straightaway. To impose it across the entire screen, you will have to click in the right-hand box (one of Apple's less intuitive ideas) and… Voilà!

This control panel can also be used to change the (here's some Macspeak) 'blinking rate of the insertion point' – the insertion point is the vertical bar you see in text documents – from medium, to fast or slow. Just click one of the three buttons.

Menu Blinking (the number of times a pull-down menu selection blinks to confirm that it has been selected), and the Alarm Clock's day, date and time can be reset from here in a similar way.

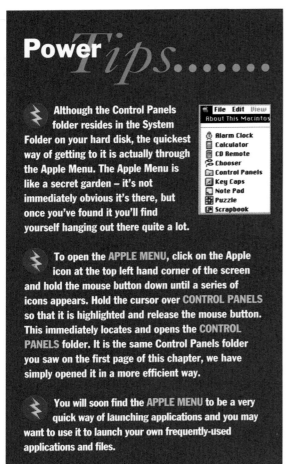

Although the Control Panels folder resides in the System Folder on your hard disk, the quickest way of getting to it is actually through the Apple Menu. The Apple Menu is like a secret garden – it's not immediately obvious it's there, but once you've found it you'll find yourself hanging out there quite a lot.

To open the APPLE MENU, click on the Apple icon at the top left hand corner of the screen and hold the mouse button down until a series of icons appears. Hold the cursor over CONTROL PANELS so that it is highlighted and release the mouse button. This immediately locates and opens the CONTROL PANELS folder. It is the same Control Panels folder you saw on the first page of this chapter, we have simply opened it in a more efficient way.

You will soon find the APPLE MENU to be a very quick way of launching applications and you may want to use it to launch your own frequently-used applications and files.

SOUND

One of the more enjoyable forms of work avoidance available on the Mac is the Sound control panel. This enables you to customize your Mac's Alert sound by adding your own eerie voice to the its system software.

The six sounds already included are: Droplet, Indigo, Quack, Simple Beep, Sosumi and Wild Eep. Click them if you want to find out what they sound like. They will be played at the current volume setting.

The final sound you click before closing this control panel will be the default sound alert that you will hear every time you make a wrong move, so make sure you're happy with it before you close the control panel.

Pick a sound and a volume.

To change the volume of the sound, click the Speaker Volume slider and drag it up or down. Your Mac will play the current Alert sound at the volume level you have selected.

You can also record your own personalised sounds and annoy your family and friends more than you ever thought possible.

The vast majority of Macs sold in recent years have come with small Apple microphones, as indicated by a microphone icon at the base of the control panel. If yours doesn't, it is a simple matter to plug a Mac Recorder (the name of the microphone, available from dealers) into the audio socket at the back of your Mac.

To record your own sound: click the button labelled Add. This brings up a second panel whose operation will be familiar if you've ever used a basic tape recorder. Click on Record and record your ten-second message.

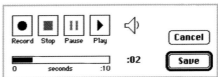

Click Stop, and that's all there is to it.

To check out your sound, hit

Record your own sound for your Mac alerts.

Play. Shout 'HAH!, that's brilliant' (everybody does) and force people to listen to it over and over again. Your digitized voice is now part of the Mac's system software.

MOUSE CONTROL

If you seem to spend half your Mac life painstakingly homing in on buttons and scroll bars because your mouse is apparently on steroids, the Mouse control panel will soon help you subdue it. Similarly, if it's too slow, you can use this control panel to speed it up.

First double click on the Mouse control panel icon. A window will open to reveal two rows of buttons.

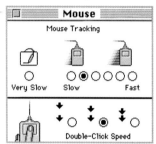

Set your own mouse speed here.

The top row is for resetting Mouse Tracking (another term for cursor movement). Clicking the 'very slow' button is really designed for use with a graphics tablet and puts your mouse on a course of sleeping tablets. This will almost certainly prove too slow. By hitting each button in turn and taking your mouse for a quick test-drive you will quickly find a speed you are comfortable with. The second row of buttons enables you to slow down, or otherwise redefine your Mac's double-clicking speed. This enables you to launch applications at your own pace until you've got the hang of rapid clicking.

BRIGHTNESS CONTROL

Many Macs have brightness and contrast controls on the front of the monitor. For those that don't, Apple has provided a basic brightness control panel. To access it, select Control Panels from the pull-down Apple menu to the top left of your screen. Double click on the Brightness control panel and use the slider to make adjustments.

COLOUR CONTROL

This control panel is used to change the colour of window borders and the highlight colour used to point out selected text. To launch it, double click on the Colour control panel. The panel opens to reveal two pull-down menus. Select a colour from the choice available in each, and a corresponding change to your window borders and highlighter will take effect immediately.

You can even re-define the way that your Mac displays its windows with this panel.

VIEWS

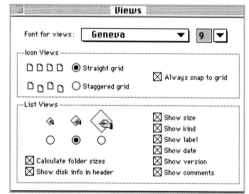

The Views control panel enables you to customize the way your folders appear and to increase the amount of information displayed when you View folders by name. To launch the Views control panel, select Control Panels from the pull down Apple Menu at the top left-hand corner of the screen. Then double click on Views.

Showing all the info possible will slow you down.

Now, by clicking in every check box you can force your Mac to display: the size of every file; the file type of every file (application, word-processing document etc); its label; the date it was last modified; its version number if it is an application; and any comments you may have attached to a file.

Name	Size	Kind	Label	Last Modified	Version	Comments
*copy820	87K	folder	–	Wed, May 19, 1993, 10:35 am	–	
*COPY910	108K	folder	–	Wed, May 19, 1993, 10:50 am	–	
911*COPY	111K	folder	–	Mon, Jun 14, 1993, 8:37 pm	–	
916*COPY	104K	folder	–	Sat, Jul 24, 1993, 10:07 pm	–	
917*COPY	102K	folder	–	Mon, Aug 9, 1993, 12:25 am	–	
COPY821	110K	folder	–	Wed, May 19, 1993, 10:35 am	–	
COPY822	116K	folder	–	Wed, May 19, 1993, 10:35 am	–	
COPY823	111K	folder	–	Wed, May 19, 1993, 10:48 am	–	
COPY824	116K	folder	–	Wed, May 19, 1993, 10:48 am	–	
COPY825	120K	folder	–	Wed, May 19, 1993, 10:48 am	–	
COPY901	57K	folder	–	Wed, May 19, 1993, 10:48 am	–	
COPY902	zero K	folder	–	Wed, May 19, 1993, 10:49 am	–	
COPY903	111K	folder	–	Wed, May 19, 1993, 10:49 am	–	
COPY904	116K	folder	–	Wed, May 19, 1993, 10:49 am	–	
COPY905	128K	folder	–	Wed, May 19, 1993, 10:49 am	–	

Get the the full low-down on your Mac's contents at a glance.

33

Control Freaks

You can make files snap to an invisible grid, either straight or staggered – this will only be noticeable when you are viewing files by icon – and you can change the size and style of the typeface used to list files and applications. This is especially useful for users with poor eyesight. For example, selecting 24 point Times has an interesting effect on labels attached to the hard disk and Wastebasket icons (see the picture below), as well as all the other text fields. Pick the font that suits you best.

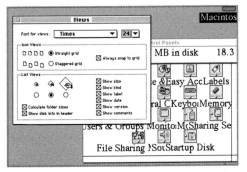

Playing around with views can lead to some fun effects.

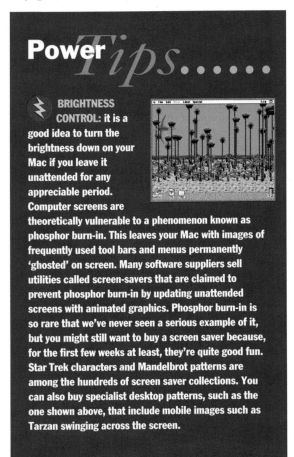

BRIGHTNESS CONTROL: it is a good idea to turn the brightness down on your Mac if you leave it unattended for any appreciable period. Computer screens are theoretically vulnerable to a phenomenon known as phosphor burn-in. This leaves your Mac with images of frequently used tool bars and menus permanently 'ghosted' on screen. Many software suppliers sell utilities called screen-savers that are claimed to prevent phosphor burn-in by updating unattended screens with animated graphics. Phosphor burn-in is so rare that we've never seen a serious example of it, but you might still want to buy a screen saver because, for the first few weeks at least, they're quite good fun. Star Trek characters and Mandelbrot patterns are among the hundreds of screen saver collections. You can also buy specialist desktop patterns, such as the one shown above, that include mobile images such as Tarzan swinging across the screen.

LABELS

If you're unhappy with the choice of labels available to you in the Label menu, you can change both the colour and the label, from the Labels control panel. To launch Labels, select Control Panels from the pull down Apple menu at the top left-hand corner of your screen. Then double click on the Labels icon.

To change the way labels read first highlight one and then type in a more apposite label; change 'Personal' to 'Letters', for example. A single click on the colour box reveals a colour wheel with which you can change the label's colour.

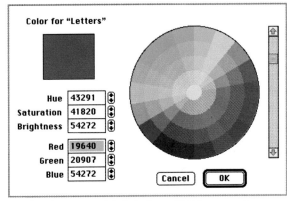

Altering the way your labels looks couldn't be any easier.

As as side issue, if you don't see the point in labels, type in any message you like, from a pithy epithet to a set of reminders! Before you attach a label to a file, first make sure you are in the Finder clicking on the hard disk. If you are, you will see the Mac icon in the Application menu at the top right-hand corner of the screen. The active window – the one with the solid stripy border around it – will be either a folder or a drive, not a document.

If you are not in the Finder, and you own a Performa, you may find you are not able to see your hard disk icon and you will have to select Finder from the Application menu.

34

Once in the Finder, select the applications or files you want to label by clicking them, then pull down the Label menu. Select a label by highlighting it and releasing the mouse button and it will be attached to each selected file. The file's icon should change colour immediately.

No matter where this file (or files) disappears to in its future life on your Mac, you will always be able to call it to heel by selecting 'by Label' from the View menu.

DATE AND TIME CONTROL

If your Mac is behind the times, you can quickly bring it up to date using the Date and Time control panel. First double click on the Control Panels folder, inside the System Folder on the hard disk. Double clicking on the Date and Time control panel icon brings up two simple buttons and displays.

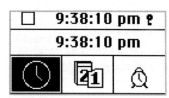

Stay on time with this control panel.

Click on any figure in the date or time displays and it will become highlighted and two small arrows will appear. Click on these arrows to adjust the highlighted figure up or down. If you want to customize the format of date and time displays (separating day/month/year by slashes instead of commas, say), then hit one of the format buttons. A simple dialog box appears, allowing you to select from a range of separators.

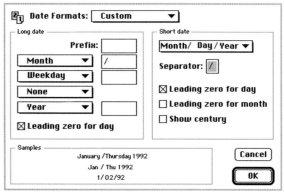

Don't be saddled with the same old time and date formats.

If, alas, you want to do something more useful such as install your Mac clock permanently in the menu bar then you will tinker with this control panel in vain. This effect can only be achieved using an add-in control panel, or CDEV such as *SuperClock*, which you have to buy separately and install yourself. Installing control panels or any other system-level item such as a font, utility or extension is very easy in System 7. You simply drag its icon onto the unopened icon of the System Folder and the Mac puts it away automatically.

To display the less rarefied clock that comes with your Mac, and to set a simple alarm, click on the Apple icon at the top left-hand corner of your screen and pull down the Apple menu until Alarm Clock is selected. Then let go. If the clock box is only partially displayed, click on the lever at the right-hand side to open it. The box that appears should show the correct time and date, in the format you selected earlier.

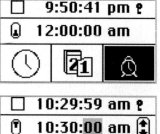

What time is it? Your Mac can tell you. After you've told it that is.

To set an alarm, click on the small 'alarm clock' icon. This displays the current alarm setting in the centre row. Click on the hours, minutes and seconds in turn, using the up and down arrows to set the alarm time.

Then click the button on the left of the alarm to prime it, making sure you deselect any highlighted areas, otherwise the alarm may not go off. Cross your fingers – your alarm is now set.

This somewhat elaborate procedure has the vaguely anti-climactical effect of triggering your current alert sound and producing a flashing alarm clock icon where the Apple icon usually is. Big Deal.

The Alarm Clock and all the other mini applications you see when you pull down the Apple Menu are known as desktop accessories or DAs. You will find them by double clicking first on the System Folder and then on the Apple Items Menu folder, inside.

Click to select the Alarm Clock icon and pull down the File menu until Make Alias is highlighted. Now drag a copy into the Startup Items folder, and/or onto the desktop, and that's all there is to it.

Every time you start your Mac from now on the Alarm Clock will be one of the first things you see. Follow this same procedure to make frequently used applications, such as word processors or spreadsheets, appear automatically on startup.

If you subsequently want to prevent an application launching at startup, drag its Alias out of the Startup Items Folder.

PERFORMA ALERT

If your Mac is a Performa, only one application window is usually displayed at a time, even when there are several applications running. This has the unfortunate side-effect that when you restart your Mac, the ALARM CLOCK and other Startup items will be visible, but the FINDER, together with your hard disk, and other desktop paraphernalia, all seem to have vanished.

To restore your desktop, select FINDER from APPLICATION MENU (the pull down menu at the top right-hand corner of your screen) and the Mac icon will reappear, along with your beloved hard disk.

Power Tips

DATE AND TIME To make the alarm clock appear on screen automatically every time you start up, place an Alias of it in the STARTUP ITEMS folder. An Alias is a pointer to an application or file. It is made by clicking on the designated file, and selecting Make Alias from the file menu. By making multiple Aliases you can launch frequently used applications or documents from a variety of convenient places.

SHARING AND CARING: if your Mac is part of a network (see the Sharing control panel later in this chapter) there is one major rule of etiquette that you should abide by – and that you should make others abide by too – the rule is as follows:

If you need to take a file from someone else's Mac over the network, make sure to tell them before you start to copy it (a good idea is to tell them to save what they're working on). Remember that, even though you're using the network as the information route, you are still pulling data from another person's hard disk. This action can mean that, at best, the person who's Mac you're copying from will find there mouse moving jerkily around the screen (not a good idea if you're doing detailed graphics work). At worst it could cause both yours and the other person's Mac to freeze up.

MONITORS CONTROL

Whether your Mac displays colours or shades of grey, you can alter the number of colours and shades it displays using the Monitors control panel. If you intend to use more than one monitor you will also use this panel to configure your monitors.

To launch Monitors, select Control Panels from the pull down Apple Menu to the top left of your screen, then double click on Monitors in the control panels folder.

If, like most people, you have one monitor, you will probably use this control panel only to alter the number of colours your Mac can display – when you have added more video memory, for example.

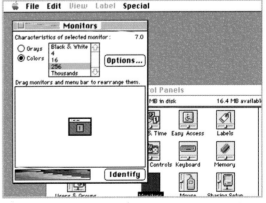

Make certain that your screen is showing the correct hues.

The buttons at the top left-hand corner of the monitors window (known as radio buttons), and the box next to them, indicate the current settings for your Mac.

The picture below indicates that 256 different colours can currently be displayed on this particular Mac screen.

Note that this does not amount to an absolute limitation on the colours this Mac can display, only on the range of colours that can be displayed at one time.

If you need a greater palette of colours, for very detailed graphic work perhaps, or for a particularly gory horror CD-ROM, click on the number of colours you need. The trade-off is that more colours require more video memory.

Many Macs come with only enough video memory for 256 colours on a 14in screen (or thousands of colours on a 12in screen – again there is a trade-off between the number of pixels available on screen and the number of colours you can display, for a given amount of video memory). If you have more than one monitor, or if you have purchased a new video-card (an ad-on device to provide better screen output for your Mac) you may need to check which monitor is running as the 'main' screen, or if your Mac has noticed the new video-card. To do this, click on the Options button in the monitors control panel. A screen like the one below will appear, this will enable you to configure your setup properly.

Do you know if you have a video card? Find out.

MEMORY CONTROL

The Memory control panel is your way of controlling how your Mac uses its RAM and hard disk. If you know the tricks of the trade you can make it perform better than you thought possible, without having to lay out more money.

You may, for example, find that your Mac frequently reminds you that memory is running low, or that there is not enough memory for one application to run, unless another is closed down.

One obvious, if expensive, solution is to go out and buy more memory. This is a good idea if you intend working regularly with high resolution graphics files, powerful image manipulation programs, large databases or spreadsheets. If you want to learn how to upgrade memory, turn to Chapter 12.

However, if the memory shortfall is only an occasional problem, a more economical solution is to adjust the way your Mac uses the RAM it already has.

Virtual memory is not real memory. It is space on your hard disk – a much slower medium – that can be configured to act like random access memory (RAM). This is a very powerful feature. Your Mac has at least 40Mb of hard disk space, and if you turned it all over to RAM, you would have more memory than most professional graphic designers.

Such a drastic allocation is, of course, not practical, as you need your hard disk to store applications and files, and applications would run very slowly on such a system.

Instead, you should use virtual memory sparingly, and only occasionally, to give you extra application space when you need it. Switch virtual memory on by clicking the (radio) button as shown here.

If you have more than one hard drive then you will be able to choose which drive provides the 'extra virtual RAM' from the pull down menu. The two text fields tell you how much real RAM is currently available for you to use and how much storage you have spare on the chosen hard drive.

Experiment with different values of virtual memory – sticking approximately to the default figure suggested by your Mac – using the up and down arrows.

The picture below illustrates to an exaggerated degree what can be achieved using virtual memory, with three large applications running simultaneously. Remember that this is only a 5Mb machine.

Control Freaks

Once again you are advised to use this feature sparingly, and to buy more RAM if you regularly need this kind of application space.

32-bit addressing is a way of working with data that allows your Mac to access more than 8Mb of memory.

If you have installed more than 8Mb, the first thing you should do is turn 32-bit addressing on.
A common problem that occurs when users install extra memory is that if you don't switch on 32-bit addressing your Mac won't know it's there and your expensive investment is being wasted.

It may seem a bit ridiculous that there is button hidden away in your Mac's control panels that has to be switched on to make your Mac work properly, especially when Apple could so easily build a machine that does it automatically. The reason for this is that not all applications work well under 32-bit addressing, and some of the less mainstream ones may even cause your system to crash.

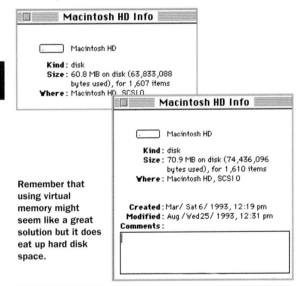

Remember that using virtual memory might seem like a great solution but it does eat up hard disk space.

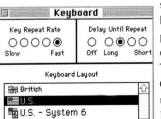

DON'T PANIC

This is one of Mac's tetchiest control panels. If you don't know your RAM from your ROM and don't want to learn, PANIC NOW and skip to the next section. But if you feel you have the patience and want to know how to squeeze the last drop of oomph out of you Mac, read on.

If you experience regular system crashes (everything freezes up and you see the sad Mac icon, and will be unable to restart your Mac without switching it off), you should either switch 32-bit addressing off, wasting your expensive RAM, or replace the offending application with one of the great many that have been designed to work with 32-bit addressing. Such applications are said to be '32-bit clean'.

Disk cache is the small chunk of memory which your Mac sets aside to help applications run faster. It does this by providing a local place for your Mac to store frequently used information which saves a great deal of fetching and carrying from the much slower hard disk. In the example you will see that the cache size is set to 128K. This is about one fiftieth of the total memory available on this Mac and is a perfectly reasonable overhead for the performance gains it brings.

Increasing this disk cache may bring further improvements in your Mac's performance, but if at the same time it prevents a single application from launching you may think it too much. Experiment with a range of disk cache settings up to around 250K using the up and down arrows in the scroll bar, until you find the one that works best with the applications you use.

STARTUP DISK

The Startup Disk control panel lets you choose the default or startup disk which will boot up your Mac. It is only relevant if you have several drives connected to your Mac. Most users will have only one.

KEYBOARD CONTROL

The Keyboard control panel allows you to alter the keyboard layout to choose between UK and US keyboard layouts. On a British keyboard, for example, when you simultaneously press Shift and 3, you will produce the symbol £. On a US keyboard these keys produce the symbol # on screen.

To launch it, select Control Panels from the pull down Apple Menu to the top left of your screen. Then double click on the Keyboard control panel.

This panel also enables you to alter the rate at which characters repeat when a key is held down, and also the delay that occurs before characters start to repeat. Simply click a button.

In this way awkward typists can avoid accidentally generating repeat characters and fast typists can work as quickly as they like.

MAP CONTROL

The Map control panel is actually more of a utility than a control panel. It doesn't change the way you work with your Mac. It pinpoints the cities of the world by their longitude and latitude, and tells you the time there. If this doesn't seem very useful, that's because it isn't. We've never met anybody who knows anybody who ever heard of anyone who had used this control panel. The idea is that by selecting a city and clicking the button marked Set, the internal clock inside your Mac instantly changes to the local time. Useful only if you're

lugging your Mac around the world with you, or if you do a great deal of trans-continental telephone work. Aside from that however, you can give this one a miss unless you're travelling with a PowerBook, one of Apple's portable computer range.

EASY ACCESS CONTROL

For people who find the basic controls of their machine physically too awkward to master, Apple has laid on a number of features, called Easy Access, that provide alternative ways for interacting with the Mac.

Sticky Keys, for example, allows you to perform shortcuts – alternatives to menu commands that use multiple key combinations – without having to press all 80 keys simultaneously.

Power *Tips*........

To find out how much memory your Mac currently has, and how it's being used, click on the hard drive to make sure you are in the Finder, then on the APPLE MENU at the top left-hand corner of your screen, and select ABOUT THIS MACINTOSH from the pull down menu. The total system memory is indicated. 4M (Megabyte) or 5M is standard on most Macs and is a reasonable amount of memory to work with most mainstream applications. The horizontal bar charts indicate the amount of the total memory that is being used by the system software – the software that makes your Mac work – and how much by individual applications. As you can see from the example, even with only one application running, the largest block of unused memory is only 1M. In other words, your memory is already almost totally used up. If you want to occasionally run another one or two applications, you will have to put your memory to more effective use.

To make more effective use of your memory, first select CONTROL PANELS from the pull down APPLE MENU to the top left of your screen. Then double click on the MEMORY icon in the control panels folder. You will be presented with possibly the most esoteric of all the Mac's controls. Don't panic – you are well on your way to mastering one of the most powerful tools available on your Mac!

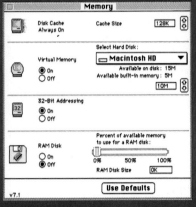

Keep an eye on what your Mac is doing with its memory resources at all time.

Mouse Keys enables you to control the cursor using the numeric keypad instead of the mouse.

And Slow Keys is designed to allow slow and awkward typists to type slowly and awkwardly without registering a lot of accidental keystrokes.

To switch on Sticky Keys, press the Shift Key five times without moving the mouse. The icon pictured below appears at the top right hand corner of the screen and is accompanied by an ascending scale which tells you are in Sticky Keys heaven.

Under normal circumstances, keyboard shortcuts are used by more experienced Mac users to help them work more quickly.

Typing Command and W together, for example, will immediately close the currently active window, saving users from homing in with the cursor.

To type the same combination using Sticky Keys you need to hit the modifier key (either Command, Shift, Option or Control) – an arrow will now appear above the Sticky Keys icon to indicate that a modifier has been selected. Then you need to hit the character key required for the job in hand – in this case W – and the window will close. Hit Shift five times more to turn Sticky Keys off.

To switch on Mouse Keys, press Command–Shift–Clear (Clear is in the top row of the numeric keypad) and an ascending scale from the Mac's built-in speaker tells you Mouse Keys is active. (Repeating the sequence turns Mouse Keys off again, to the accompaniment of a descending scale.) Press 4, and the cursor now inches minutely to the left, 6 makes it go to the right, 8 vertically up, 2 vertically down, 7 diagonally upwards to the left, and so on.

To switch on Slow Keys (an ideal boost for novice typists), hold the Return key down for around 4 seconds. A series of rapid bleeps indicates Slow Keys is active. You can now type as slowly as you like and only the most deliberate keystrokes will be registered.

All of these features are useful in their own right, however, you can finely tune them to your own needs by using yet another control panel – this one is called Easy Access.

To launch Easy Access, first select Control Panels from the pull down Apple Menu at the top left of your screen. Then double click on the Easy Access icon.

The second picture shows the controls at their most exaggerated, with Sticky Keys on, and Slow Keys set to its slowest setting. You may find these settings make your Mac impossibly cumbersome. Experiment with this control panel until you find the combination that suits you best.

Easy Access: the control panel written for the novice typist (most of us!).

SHARING SETUP

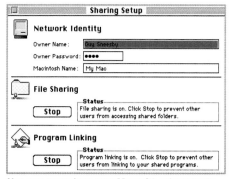

If you are attached to a network, the Sharing Setup control panel will enable you to share your files and folders with other users, allowing them to open your folders and files as if they were their own.

To launch Sharing Setup, select Control Panels from the Apple Menu and then double click on the Sharing Setup icon. Enter your name and a password. This password is the one you will use to log onto your own machine from someone else's Mac. You can even log on remotely (if you have Apple Remote Access), using a modem as long as you know the password, so make sure it is one you will be able to remember.

You can even share your Mac with other people.

Assuming that you will want to share files (or occasionally applications) with other people, hit the FileSharing button.

Next launch the Users and Groups control panel from the Control Panels folder to define which users will be allowed access to your valuable data.

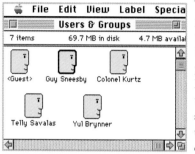

Pick your friends and neighbours here.

To grant access privileges to users, select New User from the pull down File Menu and a new user icon will appear. Then type in the name of the new user's Mac. To set a new user's password, double click on the user icon and the following window will appear. Now type in the new user's password (it is best to let them choose because, again, it is they who will have to remember it). This is the password

And make sure they know their privileges.

they will use to log onto your Mac. Finally, click on the drive or the folder you wish to share and select Sharing from the File menu. You can share your entire hard disk, a specific group of folders or even a single file; it's completely up to you, but whatever you do, you shouldn't underestimate the importance of this decision.

You can share programs or entire disks but be careful.

Power*Tips*.......

Another effective way of working with memory-hungry applications with limited RAM, is to cut down the amount of memory each application sets aside for itself, when it is launched.

To do this, first make sure you are in the Finder by clicking on your hard drive (the Finder icon should be displayed at the application menu in the top right-hand corner of the screen). Select an application which usually requires a lot of RAM, typically one which reminds you of your memory limitations when you try to launch it, by clicking on it once. Then select Get Info from the pull down File menu.

Be sure to click on the application itself, rather than the application folder (the application folder holds the application and its support files). If you have accidentally selected the folder, instead of the application within the folder, the option to reset minimum memory size does not become available.

The highlighted area in the picture indicates the minimum memory in which the application can be enticed to run. By resetting this figure so that it is lower than the preferred size, the application will run on systems with fairly limited memory. As more memory becomes available, the application will set it aside until it reaches its preferred size, when it should run more or less perfectly.

This feature, especially when used in conjunction with virtual memory, allows you to run quite powerful applications on fairly basic systems.

The downside is that the application may not run smoothly and may even cause the occasional system crash, bringing with it the inevitable loss of unsaved data. If an application crashes consistently, there are only two alternatives. One is to allocate more memory using the Get Info panel – even if this means you have to buy extra RAM. The other is to find a less voracious application to do the same job.

41

Control Freaks

Sharing only a limited range of folders, for example, means that you can be sure no-one will see those embarrassing love letters you have hidden in the depths of the hard drive, in a folder cunningly labelled 'Don't Read Me'. For similar reasons, you probably wouldn't want to share a folder called 'Expense Fiddles' to a user in your company's accounts department. A simple rule is: if you don't want to share it with everyone, don't share it with anyone.

After clicking on the folder(s) you do wish to share – you're certain now? – select Sharing from the pull down File Menu.

Click on the check box at the top of the panel on the screen, and the selected folder and all its contents will be shared. Use the lower check boxes to define which users or groups get access privileges to read and write to this folder.

When your Mac asks you whether you want to save your new access privileges click OK.

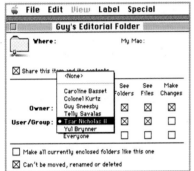

You've chosen the other people who can log onto your Mac. You don't need to worry about this again – unless you want to add a new user, or remove an old, unwanted one.

File Sharing is now set up and registered users with right access privileges can now log onto your shared files from

the the Chooser. (See Chooser in Chapter 4). Whenever another user logs onto a shared folder you will see this icon.

SHARING MONITOR CONTROL

Just because you have file sharing switched on (see Sharing Setup above), does not mean you have given over all rights to your own data. The Sharing Monitor control panel is designed to enable you to see who is checking out your important data.

Select this control panel by double clicking on Sharing Monitor in the usual way; its simple display

shows you at a glance which users are logged onto your Mac and gives an indication of their level of activity. If an unwelcome user has somehow managed to log on, or a registered user is moving large amounts of data back and forth causing your own applications to slow down, you have only to click on their name in the right-hand window and hit Disconnect and they will immediately be logged off.

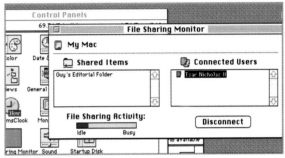

Make sure that people are not abusing their privileges here.

NUMBERS CONTROL

The Numbers control panel allows you to alter the way numbers are displayed, and the default currency symbol used (£ or $). It consists of a few straightforward pull downs and buttons.

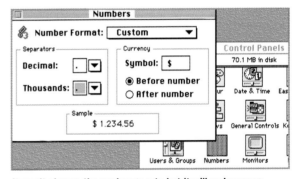

It won't change the exchange rate but it will make sense.

MISCELLANEOUS

All Macs are good machines, but not all Macs were created equal. While the majority come with Memory, Views,. Labels, General and the other standard panels, some Macs feature an idiosyncratic control panel or three for controlling features unique to their particular model or range. Opening up the Control Panels folder and taking a look at what's there is your best way of finding out. However, here are a few examples: if your Mac is a Performa, for example, it will have an At Ease control panel. This is used for turning the simplified interface on

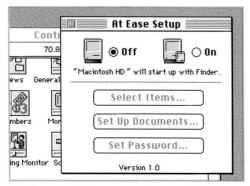

Keeping unwanted users away is easy with At Ease.

and off. We strongly recommend that, unless you have a specific requirement for At Ease – for example, your Mac is being used by a number of inexperienced or potentially unreliable or mischievous users – a classroom full of children perhaps – you should leave it permanently switched off.

A Performa will also have a control panel for PC Exchange. PC Exchange is a straightforward utility for painlessly reading disks created on the normally non-Mac compatible IBM PC and clones. Not only will you be able to read from a PC-disk, you will also able to edit the documents on it. This control panel enables you to control which Mac application will be brought to bear on each particular type of PC file. Turn to Chapter 5 to see this utility in action.

Equally individual are Macs with CD-ROM drives built in. These come equipped with control panel called Apple CD Speed Switch that is used for switching between the drive's two speeds.

The Text control panel, on Macs where mixed scripts, such as Hebrew and Roman, are in common use, is designed so that users can choose the way fundamentally different scripts are handled, and the PowerBook control panel, understandably enough, is for use solely with PowerBooks.

Don't worry too much about these additional panels (your manual will have information about special panels) and once you have mastered the mainstream control panels, you should have no problem with any other control panel you encounter. After all, all control panels are designed to work in pretty much the same way.

Power *Tips*......... ..

LOSING CONTROL: the idea behind control panels is that you should be able to mould your Macintosh to your needs and your desire.

You should be able to alter all the parameters, the looks and the sounds of your Macintosh without causing any problems.

...HOWEVER... playing around too much can leave you with a screen full of labelled windows, ladened with 24-point Garamond text in multi-hued boxes, with squawks (or worse, your own voice screaming insane 'Hah! I've done it!') messages at you every time you attempt to press a (Sticky) key or move your mouse at a reasonable speed.

If this happens, stay calm and remember that you can always go back to the control panels and alter their set-ups back to the calm – if dull – defaults. The key here is to remember that you are in control.

SAVE OUR SYSTEM: when altering the views you are going to use with your system, keep one thing in mind – every font, window, icon or pattern you put in screen has to be drawn and re-drawn by the system. The more you ask it to do, the more your Mac will slow down as the poor, overworked system spends its valuable time making re-draws. So, if you want a less customized, but speedier, Mac try the following: Geneva as your Views font. Nine point as the font size. Don't ask for 'Folder sizes' to be calculated (this can take ages) and don't 'view by icon' (this means additional redraw time, especially if you're working in more than simple black and white).

DON'T PANIC

It is almost impossible to confuse your Mac by playing around with these few buttons and sliders.

The Apple Menu

order up your favourite items

A La Carte

4

The Apple Menu is the repository for two very powerful system tools and half a dozen utilities that Apple ships free with your system. It lurks under the Apple icon at the top left-hand corner of your screen and is available to you from within any application.

THE APPLE MENU

The Apple Menu is the repository for two very powerful system tools and half a dozen utilities that Apple ships free with your system. It lurks under the Apple icon at the top left-hand corner of your screen and is available to you from within any application.

The best way of thinking about the Apple Menu is as a mini-launchpad for these system-altering tools known as the Chooser and Control Panels, as well as a storehouse for your own favourite gadgets, utilities, applications, files and toys. It is easy to install files and applications here, and everything in the Apple Menu can be launched with a single flourish of the mouse.

To open the Apple Menu, click on the Apple icon at the top left-hand corner of the screen and hold the mouse button down. The menu will scroll down to reveal a series of icons often referred to as desktop accessories or DAs.

Seven are fairly useful, if hardly magnificent, utilities laid on by Apple.

Two, the Chooser and Control Panels, are a good deal

more powerful and, if you intend to get the most out of your Mac, you are likely to have numerous dealings with them.

Starting at the top of the Apple Menu, the first DA you come to is the Alarm Clock.

ALARM CLOCK

Select the Alarm Clock and a box displaying the time, day and date immediately appears. This very basic utility also enables you to set a rudimentary alarm. To launch the Alarm Clock, select it from the pull-down Apple Menu at the top left of the screen and the window shown here will appear.

If you don't see the whole window, click on the lever towards the top right-hand corner to open it up fully.

To alter the time, click on the large clock icon. Then click on either the hours, minutes or seconds field, in the second row, depending on which you want to alter. Type in the new improved digits using the keyboard or use the two arrows to scroll up and down.

To reset the date, you must click on the calendar icon in the bottom row, and scroll in the same way.

To set an alarm, click on the alarm clock icon and select a time. Then click on the switch icon that appears to the left of the second row to prime the alarm to go off.

When the Alarm sounds, it will play your current Alert Sound (see Chapter 3, Sound Control Panel) and flash an alarm clock icon in place of the Apple icon at the top left-hand side of the screen.

Be sure not to leave any fields highlighted or this pernickety utility will not work properly.

CALCULATOR

Calculator is a basic four-function program that comes in very useful for adding, multiplying, dividing and subtracting numbers. Launch it from within any other application and type figures directly from the keyboard or click on the Calculator keypad.

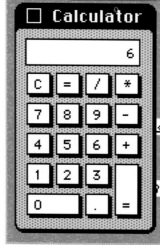

Answers can be copied and pasted from the calculator to a document.

This is great for slightly tricky arithmetic, reports, quick calculations.

Your Mac comes with its own calculator built-in.

CD REMOTE – AUDIO CD

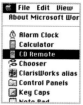

If your Mac has a built-in CD-ROM drive, or you've added an external CD-ROM player yourself, the CD Remote DA will appear in the Apple Menu. This DA allows you to play audio CDs on the Mac.

It features the same basic controls you would expect to find on the front panel of a hi-fi CD player, including fast forward, scan, skip and infinite replay. Basically, it enables you to put any audio CD into the Mac's caddy and play back the sounds as you would with a standard CD.

Your Mac CD is simplicity itself.

THE CHOOSER

Configure your printer, log onto other Macs and much more…

In its simplest sense, the Chooser is a navigation device. It allows you to set up your printer, or choose from a number of printers connected to your Mac. For networked users, it also allows you to chart any path through the many arcane devices that at one time or another may find themselves attached to your Mac.

Specifically, the Chooser provides a direct line to printers and modems connected to your Mac's two serial ports (the sockets at the back of your machine with printer and telephone icons) to printers connected to the SCSI port, and to any other networked devices and services.

For the vast majority of un-networked users, this adds up to a single dedicated printer.

Launch the Chooser by selecting it from the Apple Menu and a window that looks like one of these will appear.

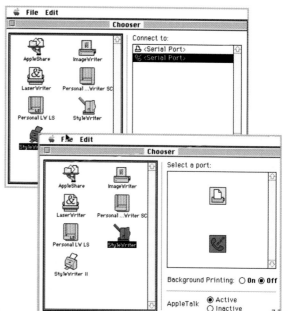

Prepare to choose your printer from this easy set-up screen.

Select the appropriate printer model by clicking on its icon (the printer's icon will appear here automatically once you have installed the driver). Two icons, representing the modem port and the printer port, will now appear in the right-hand screen, prompting you for information about which port you connected the printer to.

Click on the appropriate icon, and then close the Chooser window.

Finally, select Page Setup from the pull-down File menu to tell your Mac you're happy with the printer set up, then click OK. That's as difficult as it usually gets.

Configuring a modem is a very similar procedure and in each case, the manufacturer will provide full step-by-step instructions.

WORKING IN GROUPS

If you work as part of a networked group, and share devices as well as information across an AppleTalk or Ethernet network, you will probably have a great many more dealings with the Chooser.

Setting up and administering a network is a job for a network administrator, and is not covered in this book. But once you are connected, there are a few tricks you can learn to make the most of your connected status, such as logging onto other Macs.

Select AppleShare from the Chooser, and each AppleShare zone (discrete work group areas on the network set up by the system administrator) appears in the lower left-hand window.

Click on a zone and the Mac will prompt you for a file server from the right–hand window. A file server is just a term for a storage area within a zone where shared information is kept. This could be anything from a dedicated server machine, locked away in an attic somewhere, to your neighbour's Mac. It doesn't matter. The important thing is that all this precious information is now available to you.

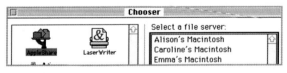

Click to select a file-server. If you are asked for a password, enter it. If you don't have a password, you may not be authorised to access this server.

In the next screen you may also be offered a subset of the file server you have selected, a bit like Russian dolls in that you can have a file-server within a file-server within an AppleShare zone. Click on one, and finally its icon will appear on the desktop. You can now access any (unlocked) folders and files on this volume by double clicking in the usual way.

From the Chooser, it is also possible for you to log onto another user's hard disk, and open and copy files directly from there, if they have set up their Macs for 'sharing' and given you access privileges. Other users' Macs appear in the same Chooser window as any other file-server.

If you want to share information by publishing your own hard drives, you can do so by turning on file sharing, using the Sharing Setup control panel in the Control Panels folder. (See Sharing Setup, Chapter 3)

CONTROL PANELS

Selecting Control Panels from the Apple menu opens a folder which, as the name suggests, contains a number of control panels that allow you to really get under the hood of your Mac and make it work for you, rather than against you. For a full explanation of how each control panel works, turn to Chapter 3.

THE NOTEPAD

The Notepad is a simple but effective utility for leaving messages for family and friends, jotting down rough notes, jogging your memory or making lists on the spur of the moment. Note Pad is a no thrills single-font eight-page scratchpad. To use it, just select Note Pad from the Apple menu and start typing away.

Anything you type is automatically saved, and will be there when you start your Mac up again.

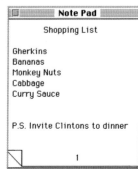

You needn't bother with sticky yellow notes any more.

KEY CAPS

Key Caps is a powerful utility that provides a window on the host of typographical characters that are available on your Mac but don't appear on the regular keyboard. To find them and use them in your documents, launch Key Caps by selecting it from the Apple Menu. Select the font you intend to use in your document from the pull down Key Caps menu.

Now experiment by pressing various combinations of modifier keys (Option, Shift and Ctrl) and you will see that for each font there is quite a large collection of typographical characters available to you.

It might not look like much, but this screen is incredibly handy.

Each font has its own subtly different selection of typographical characters. Selecting Helvetica, for example, and pressing Option, allows you to produce any of the characters shown below.

Discover the secrets of your Mac's keyboard with Key Caps.

Selecting a different modifier key will produce a slightly different selection and selecting a different typeface will produce another selection still. Experiment with different fonts and combinations of the Option, Shift and Ctrl keys until you find the character or characters you want.

Once you have found a character, there are two ways of inserting it into a document.

The first is to generate the character on the Key Caps

All Greek to you? Don't worry, all will be explained...

Power *Tips*........

The City or place name fonts installed on your Mac (Chicago, Geneva, Monaco and New York) each have their own portfolio of special characters. Try selecting 6pt Geneva, New York and Monaco respectively from the Font menu, and pressing Option, Shift and ~ simultaneously – you will see a host of strange, non-alphabet characters appearing on your screen. By using the different key combinations and experimenting with point sizes, you can create many, many weird and wonderful characters to spice up your own Mac work.

These characters can be used to add impact to documents, but only if you intend outputting them to QuickDraw printers, such as the Apple ImageWriter or Stylewriter range. These special characters will not output correctly to laser printers or image setters – you will need to use special character sets, or even EPS (Encapsulated PostScript files) if you want to obtain similar effects at the high-end.

If you are interested in learning the decidedly arcane reasons why some fonts won't work on some output devices, turn to Chapter 5 for more information on fonts and printing.

HINT Try not to use City fonts if you are outputting to a laser printer or imagesetter.

ACCENTS To type a character with a diacritical mark, such as an acute or grave accent, press Option and the special key together, and then type the character:

GRAVE ACCENT (à,è) type Option ` then the character

ACUTE ACCENT (á,é,í,ó,ú) type Option e then the character

CIRCUMFLEX (â,ê,î,ô,û) type Option i then the character

Tilde (ñ) type Option n then the character

UMLAUT (ä,ë,ï,ö,ü) type Option u then the character

CEDILLA (ç) type Option c

key pad, copy it from the Key Caps display, by highlighting copy from the pull down Edit menu, and then pasting it to the document in the usual way.

The alternative is to use Key Caps as an incredibly useful, on-line reference to the typographical internals of your Mac. Experiment until you find the key combination that produces the required character, and then return to your document and hit the same key combination. The character will appear as advertised.

The following characters were created using the same keystrokes (Option and then every key on the keyboard in turn) but in two different fonts.

`¡™£¢∞§¶•ªºº–≠œ∑´®†¥¨^øπåß∂ƒ©∆¬…æΩ≈ç√∫~µ≤ ≥ *Helvetica*

ℑ♠≤'⁰⁄ƒ∞≈......∠↑∉•↔◆ ×←⊥↓≠ ♣∂⊗♥∅ℜ⊃—|⊕ ℘ ≡~"≥ *Symbol*

There are also a number of special character fonts, available from third-party font manufacturers, that offer scalable boats, planes, cartoon characters, bullet points, asterisks – you name it – and work with any printer.

SCRAPBOOK

One of the handiest utilities in the Apple Menu, and one of the most under-used, is the Scrapbook, a storehouse for frequently used graphics, logos, letterheads and sounds. A bit like Note Pad in that whatever you paste here is automatically saved to the hard disk, Scrapbook has the advantage that it can handle a much wider range of media. It is even possible to store video sequences here if your Mac has the Apple QuickTime extension installed. (See Chapter 11 for more on working with video.)

The Scrapbook comes with a number of images and sounds already pasted into it – for example:

Alternatively you can create your own letter heading or logo in one of the many Mac drawing and painting packages available and paste it into the Scrapbook, ready to be un-leased with a flourish of your mouse on a monochrome world.

To add items to the Scrapbook, copy them by clicking to select them and using the Copy command in the pull down Edit Menu; click on the Scrapbook and select Paste in exactly the same way. (To learn more about creating and working with images and using image manipulation programs, turn to Chapter 6.)

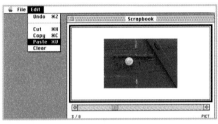

To paste your own sounds into the Scrapbook, first launch the Sound control panel. If you don't know how to use this control panel, turn to Chapter 3.

Swap pix between programs with Scrapbook.

Once you have recorded your sound and Added it to the Mac's built-in list of sound files, click on its name in the control panel and again choose Copy from the pull down Edit menu. Then click on the Scrapbook and Paste in the same way. To play back your sound, hit the Play Sound button. This is way too cool for beginners so you might want to keep a bottle of aspirin handy.

This sound can now be pasted into any sound-aware document.

PUZZLE

Wile away your spare moments with the Apple menu Puzzle. The idea is to recreate the Apple logo by clicking each element into place tile by painful tile. As you can see from the diagram to the right it's not all that easy.

PERFORMA TIP

Performa owners take note. The Apple Menu is an infinitely more compact and effective launcher than the one that annoyingly appears every time you turn on your machine. If you want to turn off the Launcher, and use the Apple Menu instead, turn to Chapter 1 to see how.

System *Tips*

To add or remove Apple Menu items, you need to locate the Apple Menu Items folder on the hard disk. Double click on the hard disk icon, and then on the System Folder icon. Then double click on the Apple Menu Items folder and you will find your self at home with the DAs.

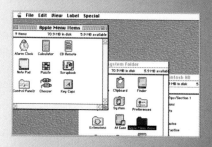

To add an application to the Apple Menu folder, one way is to simply select it from the applications folder – or wherever else you keep your applications – and drag it into the Apple Menu Items folder. However, moving folders and files around in this undisciplined way can soon lead to chaos.

A more effective way is to select the application, make an Alias of it and place the Alias in the Apple Menu Items folder.

An Alias is a pointer or signpost to an application that *acts* like the application itself. When you double click on it, the application launches. The important thing to bear in mind is that no matter how many Aliases you make, you should only ever have one copy of the original application.

To make an Alias, click once on the application you wish to signpost – for this example we'll use *ClarisWorks* – and choose Make Alias from the pull down File Menu. Immediately, an icon called *ClarisWorks Alias* appears. Drag *this* icon into the Apple Menu Items folder.

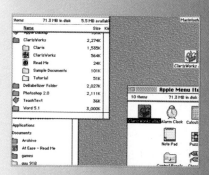

If you want a virtual copy of *ClarisWorks* on the desktop as well, make another Alias and drag it to the side of your screen. To launch *ClarisWorks* from here on in, all you have to do is select Alias from the Apple Menu or double click on one on the desktop.

The advantage of Aliases is that they give you the benefits of having multiple copies of an application, without using up vast amounts of storage, and confusing your file structure and your Mac into the bargain. You can even move the original application – even lose it – and the Alias will still be able to track it down wherever it is.

Keep all your Mac applications in one folder and then make use of the extremely useful Alias option so that you can get to the applications when and where you need them.

49

Installing
Applications

5

Most applications install on your hard disk in much the same way. The majority of applications ship (are supplied) on a number of floppy disks, which can be intimidating for the new user, but in most cases the process of installation is highly automated and merely requires someone to feed in the disks.

Here we outline the installation of a typical application. We have chosen *ClarisWorks*, because, for a number of good reasons, it features heavily in the work-thru' chapters of this book.

INSTALLING CLARIS WORKS

Installing *ClarisWorks* (and most other applications) is a simple procedure.

Take the application disks out of the sealed packet they came in. As a preliminary precaution, slide the tabs at the corner of each disk so that the holes are visible. This locks the disks and ensures they cannot be accidentally erased or overwritten.

Now insert disk 1. Double click on the Disk 1 icon and the following window will appear. Double click on the icon marked Installer. Then click OK in the installer dialog box.

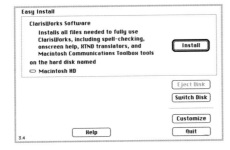

Click Install in the Easy Install dialog box and *ClarisWorks* will be copied automatically to your hard disk.

If you have other applications running, this will interfere with the installation, so the installer gives you the option of quitting all open applications, by hitting Continue, or cancelling the installation.

> **Installation on the active startup disk "Macintosh HD" cannot take place while other applications are running. Click Continue to automatically quit all other running applications. Click Cancel to leave the disk "Macintosh HD" untouched.**
>
> [Cancel] [Continue]

Hit Continue. You will be prompted to save changes to any unsaved work. Hit Yes.

From here the installer automatically takes over the show, taking information automatically from the installation disks and placing it on the hard drive in the appropriate folders. However, it needs you to feed it. Each time it spits out a disk it will ask for a specific disk to be inserted in its place. Follow the instructions until the installation is complete.

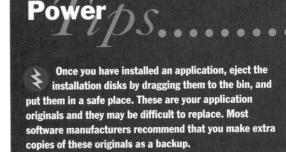

Power *Tips*............

Once you have installed an application, eject the installation disks by dragging them to the bin, and put them in a safe place. These are your application originals and they may be difficult to replace. Most software manufacturers recommend that you make extra copies of these originals as a backup.

Keep your applications in one place.

Double click on the hard disk icon and you will find a shiny new *ClarisWorks* folder waiting there for you.

Like most users, by now you have probably set up a special folder for storing your applications (see Chapter 1 if you haven't). On Performas, there is a pre-configured folder called Applications – no surprises there. Drag the *ClarisWorks* folder, which you will see on your hard disk, into the applications folder so you'll know where to find it next time you need to get at it.

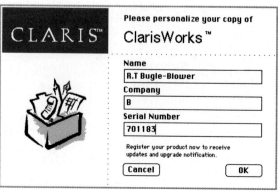

Remember that Files go into Folders.

Open the *ClarisWorks* folder by double clicking it and then double click on the *ClarisWorks* icon inside.

The first time you do so, you will be asked to personalize your copy. Key in your name, the name of your company (if relevant) and – most importantly – the registration number of your copy of *ClarisWorks*. You will find the registration number inside the registration card that came with your disks.

Fill in the details carefully. Any spelling mistakes you make now will return to haunt you every time you launch the application. Then click OK.

Installing Applications

You are now ready to do some useful work.

The first application window you see gives you a choice of six (only five in *ClarisWorks* 1.0) application categories. They are: word processing, drawing, painting, spreadsheet, database and communications.

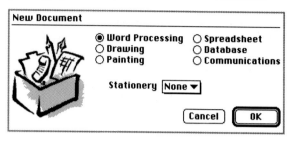

The idea of the next six chapters of this book is to demonstrate how to tackle real projects using these application environments. Many of them take *ClarisWorks* as their example, but if you can follow them, you should have no trouble getting up and running with any comparable application.

A WORD ABOUT WINDOWS

If you have a Mac Performa you are in luck. A version of *ClarisWorks* (typically *ClarisWorks* 1.0) has been pre installed on your Mac's hard disk.

Double click on the hard disk, then on the Applications folder and finally on the *ClarisWorks* folder, as shown below.

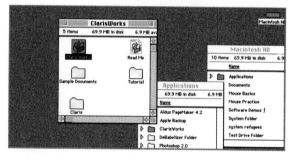

Inside the folder you will find the application itself and sundry support files and sample documents. Double click on the *ClarisWorks* icon to launch the application and then skip to one of the following application work-thru' chapters.

If you choose to upgrade to *ClarisWorks* 2.0 from 1.0 (there are many reasons to do so), simply follow the procedure outlined above to install it and save the older version to floppy disk before dragging it into the Trash.

Processed Words

In the beginning was The **Word**

6

Be not the slave of words; Fine words butter no parsnips; Don't mince my words; Words are wise men's counters; Words but wind; Idle words; Words, words, mere words.

Ninety-nine per cent of word processing files are simple one-page documents such as letters, memos and reports. Yet before you can sit down and write a simple memo, you must first wade through the wordy tome that comes with you word processor, detailing a million and one arcane features not remotely related to the work they want to do. Here we cut to the main event...

Once you become reasonably proficient in an application, a comprehensive manual is, of course, an invaluable tool. In the interim, you want to get up and running as quickly as possible, learn shortcuts as and when they are appropriate and, above all, to do some useful work.

In this chapter, you will learn how to use *ClarisWorks'* word processing environment to produce some of the most commonly used documents, such as a report, a letter, a memo and a party invitation.

You will also learn how to work with simple graphics in the word processing environment, how to mail merge a document, and how to create or customize templates for future memos and reports, which Claris refers to as stationery. The tools you will use can be found in most popular word processing packages, so you can take the skills you learn with you if you later decide to upgrade to another program. If at any time you want to print your work and skip out of the chapter, select Print from the pull-down File menu or press Command and P at the same time. When the print dialog box appears hit Print and that's all there is to it.

If you haven't set up your printer yet, turn to Chapter 11. If you want to produce a painting, a page layout, a spreadsheet, a database or a multimedia presentation or movie, skip to the appropriate chapter later in this section.

HOW TO Word Process

If you're ready to roll with a text document, the next thing to do is to launch *ClarisWorks*. Do this by double clicking the *ClarisWorks* application icon. Once you are in *ClarisWorks* select New from the pull down File menu.

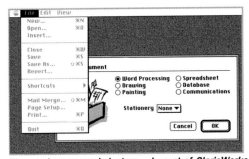

The word processor is just one element of *ClarisWorks*.

ClarisWorks defaults to the word processing application environment so you can progress from here by simply clicking OK.

You will be presented with what looks like a blank sheet of paper. That is exactly what it is. The default size of the page is US Letter (8½ in x 11 in) in the USA and A4 (8¼ in x 11⅔ in) in Europe .

You can tell where the words are going to go by the cursor.

The lightly ruled lines or page guides represent a border that forms the printable area of your report. The flashing Insertion Point at the top left-hand corner of this area indicates where any text you type will appear. If you are ready to begin your report, start typing the main body copy here. Leave any headers, footers and logos for later on.

(Remember: When you hit the right-hand page guide your text will scroll automatically to the next line. Don't hit carriage return unless you want to create a line space or start a new paragraph.)

If you make a mistake while typing, move the I-beam to the left of the text you wish to correct and, pressing the mouse key all the time, drag the I-beam until all the offending text is highlighted. Release the mouse key and simply type over the top of it.

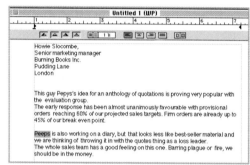

Cutting and pasting are standard tasks in most Mac programs.

You can also delete text by selecting in the same way and hitting the delete key or by moving the Insertion Point to the right of a string of characters and holding the delete key down. Remember that to move the Insertion Point you must reposition the I-beam and click the mouse button.

If you want to move a section of text, highlight it in the same way, and remove it by selecting Cut from the pull down Edit Menu.

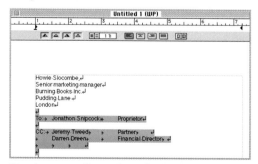

You can move entire sections of a document, not just words.

Then move the I-beam cursor to the preferred location, click to tell the Mac you want to move the Insertion Point and select Paste. If you want to move a section of text, highlight it in the same way, and copy it by selecting Cut from the pull down Edit Menu.

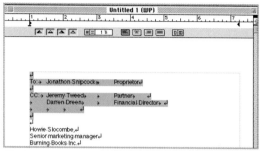

Moving sections of text for a better look is a simple task.

The best way to create a table is to use tabs. In *ClarisWorks* the default setting is for a tab at every half-inch interval. Create your table column by column, one line at a time. If the table is to be flush to the left of the document, type the first entry and then hit tab until you reach a suitable point for the start of column two. Enter the heading if there is one and repeat the procedure until you have as many columns and column headings as you require. Then hit Return. Repeat for lines two, three, four etc, using the same number of tabs between entries. Your table should always line up, even if you change the size and type of the font.

Making tables is a matter of moving tab markers to your taste.

If you want to move one part of the document above or below another, or even paste it into another document, select it by clicking and dragging the I-beam in the usual way, and press Command-X The selected text will disappear. To make it reappear elsewhere, move the I-beam to the required location, click once to create a new insertion point, and press Command-V. If you find you don't like it, repeat the procedure to put it back the way it was.

53

Power *Tips......*

One of the most powerful commands in any application is the Undo command. If, for example, you accidentally select a swathe of text and then hit delete it will disappear, but you can resurrect your work by pressing **COMMAND-Z** as long as you don't hit another key in the interim.

It is important to remember that on most programs Command-Z will undo only the last operation. Some packages have been improved to allow multiple Undos, which means you can return to any point in a session right up until your last save. However, these are few and far between and, at the time of writing, *ClarisWorks* isn't one of them.

Edit	**Format**	**Fon**
Undo Typing		**⌘Z**

If you want to see where your carriage returns and tabs have been placed, pull down the **EDIT MENU** and select **PREFERENCES**. In the dialog box that appears, click in the check box marked Show Invisibles. Alternatively, the keyboard shortcut for Show/Hide Invisibles is Command-;.

While you are here, make sure the Smart Quotes check box is also checked. This will ensure your document displays curly quotes rather than the ugly straight quotes that Mac bores always point to as evidence of Mac illiteracy.

If you want all your documents to be displayed this way, with invisibles tabs and carriage returns showing, click Make Default. If not, click OK.

Edit	**Format**	**Fon**
Undo Typing		**⌘Z**
Cut		⌘H
Copy		⌘C
Paste		**⌘U**
Clear		
Select All		**⌘A**
Insert Date		
Insert Time		
Insert Page #		
Spelling		▶
Find/Change		▶
Publishing		▶
Preferences...		
Show Clipboard		

At this stage you may be thinking the report looks a little bland and one dimensional. One way to jazz it up is to change the font, size and style of one or two of the different sections. To do so, select a text block by highlighting it in the usual way, and in turn pull down the Font, Size and Style menus. The current selection is indicated by a check mark.

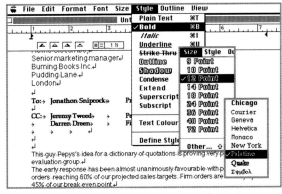

You have plenty of power to change the look of your document.

To indent a block of text, select it in the same way and drag the left indent marker in the ruler to wherever you want the indent to start. The trick with reformatting is to remember that whatever command you use applies only to the highlighted block.

The top bar lets you to set margins and tabs.

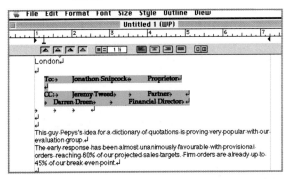

Altering the look of the text can disrupt a table, so be careful.

If you size a table up too far, or indent it too far, some words may bust through the tabs you carefully set earlier, and your table will lose shape. Adding an extra tab or two will usually set things straight.

If your report spans several pages, you might want to add a footer (or header) with the title of the report, the page number and perhaps also the date. To add a footer,

54

All the drudgery is gone...

...the work is done for you.

You think about the words.

pull down the Format menu and choose Insert Footer. Type in the name of the report and it will appear on every page.

If you want to include the date and page number, select Insert Date and Insert Page # from the pull down Edit menu. (Note: Insert Date attaches the system date to the footer so if you print the document next month, it will carry that day's date. If you want to permanently affix *today's* date, press Option at the same time as you select Insert Date.)

The Footer can be reformatted in the same as any other text by selecting the Footer and using the pull- down Font, Size and Style menus.

If you have only a 14-inch monitor (most people do) and you want to get a feel for how the whole document will look when you print it out, click on the zoom button at the bottom left-hand corner of the document window. Keep clicking until you see the whole document. Alternatively, click on

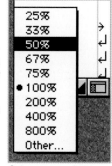

Zoom in or Zoom out.

the percentage zoom button (as shown below) and select 50%. The whole document should appear, even if the type is perhaps not particularly legible at this scale. If you don't like the way it looks, zoom in again and play around with it a bit more. To get a clearer picture turn off Invisibles by clicking the Show

Set your own view.

Invisibles check box in the Preferences dialog under the Edit menu. (Format characters, or invisibles, will not print regardless of whether you have them turned on or off.) Play around until your document looks the way you want it to.

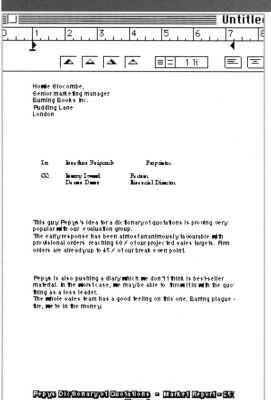

You can set-up templates for the documents that you use on a regular basis – this makes memo writing less of a chore.

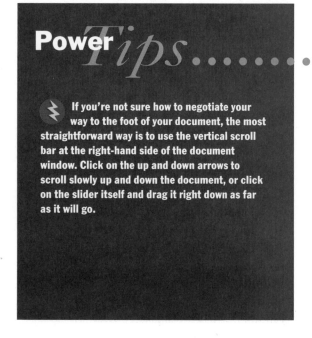

Power *Tips* . . . .

If you're not sure how to negotiate your way to the foot of your document, the most straightforward way is to use the vertical scroll bar at the right-hand side of the document window. Click on the up and down arrows to scroll slowly up and down the document, or click on the slider itself and drag it right down as far as it will go.

SOS

Save Often Stupid! This acronym takes on true meaning the first time you lose a substantial amount of work. Your Mac crashes; you select the entire document (Command-A in case you're interested) and type over the top of it; your Mac gets hit by a power failure and restarts itself. Whatever the cause, once you lose unsaved work, you have to re-enter it from scratch, even though you would rather have your tongue painted with tar.

Save your work now, by selecting Save from the pull down File menu. (Alternatively, use the keyboard shortcut, Command-S.) Something along the lines of the following dialog box will appear.

Save, save and save some more. You will hate yourself, your Mac and the rest of the world if you have to re-type two hours work again.

Notice that you can save your work in a variety of useful formats. You can, for example, save your work in *Word* 4.0 format so that it can be read by other users whose machines only have Microsoft *Word* 4.0 or 5.0. For the moment we'll content ourselves with saving in *ClarisWorks* format.

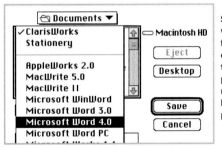

Saving your work in other formats enables you to give it to people who use different kinds of word processors.

Click Save and the document will be placed in the Documents folder, as indicated by the button at the top of the Save dialog. If you want to Save to another location, click on this button and a pull down menu will appear. From here you can choose to save to any folder

on any storage device attached to your Mac, including a floppy disk.

There are three more things you may want to do before printing out your document. The first is to spell check it. The second is to add a logo. And the third is to add outlines to parts of the document.

Spell Check

To check the spelling of your document, pull down the Edit Menu and select Spelling. Then choose Check Document from the Spelling sub menu.

Spell-checkers are really useful if you keep them tidy.

Whenever you see a triangle like this in an option in a pull down menu it means there are a number of sub menus available to you. Keep the mouse button depressed and slide the cursor over the appropriate sub menu, to highlight it, and then release.

A dialog box appears, highlighting the first 'questionable' spelling in the document. More often than not this will be a name. *ClarisWorks'* dictionary has no knowledge of the names of staff members at Burning Books Inc. and, annoyingly at first, it queries every one. Click Learn each time and these esoteric spellings will be committed to *ClarisWorks'* memory and will never be queried again, unless of course you get the spelling wrong in future.

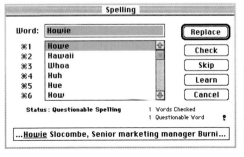

Never trust a spell-checker. They do miss things.

Click Skip if you're happy with the spelling the way it is but don't want to add the word to the Spelling dictionary.

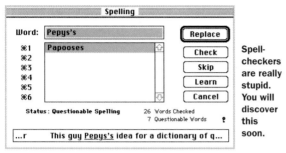

Spell-checkers are really stupid. You will discover this soon.

Once you have stepped through the entire document, correcting any genuine spelling mistakes, click Done. With *ClarisWorks* you can check an individual word for spelling in the same way;

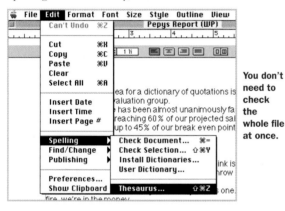

You don't need to check the whole file at once.

or you can search for an alternative using *ClarisWorks'* powerful Thesaurus.

HOW TO Select Synonyms

To use the Thesaurus, select a word by highlighting it in the usual way, and choose Thesaurus from the Spellings sub menu.

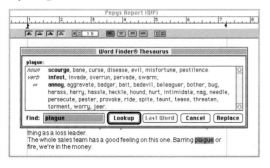

HOW TO Add Graphics

Possibly the last thing you might want to do before printing out your report is to add a graphic or logo.

Most companies have their own printed letterheaded notepaper, so pasting the company logo onto individual documents yourself may seem like an unproductive use of time. Nevertheless, some small companies don't have the volume requirement to justify printed letterheads and for others there will always come a time when you want to add some kind of graphic.It may be a graph or chart, a mugshot of a new employee for a personnel report, or a scan of a new product.

This is where *ClarisWorks* comes into its own. Most of the tools and features you have learned so far are common to leading generic packages; however, *ClarisWorks'* image-handling capability takes it, if not into a different class, then at least into a different category of software.

There are many ways of importing images to the Mac and of creating drawings and paintings yourself for that matter. There are also a great many formats in which these images can be held. The nuts and bolts of image creation, manipulation and distribution are covered in detail in Chapter 8. The creation of charts from databases and spreadsheets are covered in Chapters 9 and 10.

For the purposes of this example, we will assume the image (in this case a logo) has already been created. We will use the sample logo provided by *ClarisWorks* in the Tutorial folder. If you have access to your own company logo, across a network say or on a floppy disk, you will be able to use it in the same way.

To add a logo to the top of your report, place the

Insertion Point at the top left-hand corner of your document Now pull down the File menu and choose Insert.

You will be presented with the Insert Document dialog box. Like the Save dialog box, the Insert dialog box is a tool for navigating through the folder structure of your Mac to find a specific file or folder. It is one of the most important types of dialog box but also one of the trickiest, so if you are unsure how to use it you should make some time to go back to Chapter 1 and familiarize yourself with the way it works. For the time being, you should be able to track down the logo by taking the following steps.

Before you begin, Save your work (Command-S).

Click on the button at the top of the dialog box and a pop-up menu will appear. Select the name of your hard disk – ours is called Macintosh HD.

When the screen changes to display the contents of Macintosh HD, Select Applications.

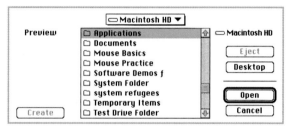

From the contents of Applications select *ClarisWorks* 2.0.

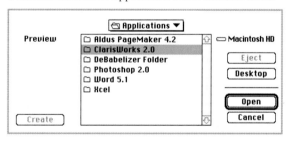

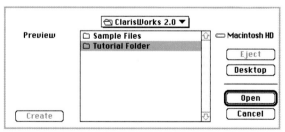

In the *ClarisWorks* 2.0 folder you will see a Tutorial folder. Click on that. Finally, click on Pegasus logo inside the Tutorial folder and click Insert, or just double click on the Pegasus logo. It will be inserted in your document at the current Insertion Point.

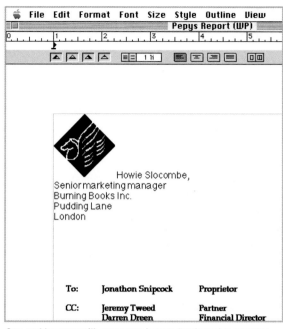

One problem you will encounter is text flowing with graphics.

Hit Return a couple of times to create some line spaces. To center the logo, select it by clicking it once and click on the Center alignment control just beneath the ruler.

A box around the logo tells you that it is selected. The square black handle allows you to stretch or otherwise distort it. You'll probably want to leave it the way it is.

There are solutions though.

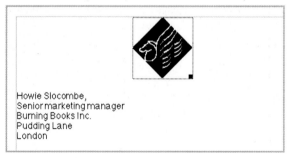

And soon you will be creating some neat documents.

Once you are happy with your document, Save it (Command-S) and press Command-P to print. If you haven't yet set your printer up properly, and you want to find out how, turn to Chapter 12.

HOW TO Create Templates

A template can be created from any Mac application in as much as a template is just a standard document, you just choose to use a regular starting point. The usual way to create a report template, say, would be to open a standard report, select Save As rather than Save from the File menu, and rename the document 'Report Template'.

Every time you subsequently wanted to write a report form, you could simply open the template, modify the appropriate sections, print it and save the changed version under a different name each time. *ClarisWorks* takes this idea of templates a step further by providing a pad of ready-to-use templates, called stationery, which can also be added to by users. These templates are conveniently located in the pull down Stationery menu that comes up as part of the furniture when you select New from the File menu.

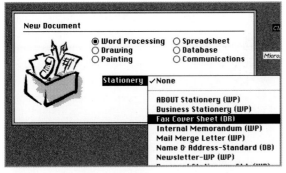

Make use of templates, they will save you loads of time.

To add a Report template to the Stationery menu, go to the place you saved your report and double click to open it, if it is not already open. Select Save As from the pull down File menu.

Rename the file clearly so it can be easily identified

You have to rename template files.

in future. Choose a simple name like 'Report Stationery'.

Select Stationery by clicking the Save As button (the one currently labelled *ClarisWorks*) and dragging the highlighting bar over the word Stationery in the pop-up menu that appears. What you have done so far is created a second document called 'Report Stationery' which you can use as a template over and over again. Hitting Save at this point would store your template in the Documents folder. Since we want the template to appear in the Stationery menu, it must be saved to the Claris Stationery folder. This is located in a Claris folder your Mac automatically placed in the System folder when the program was installed. To save your stationery to the Stationery folder, click on the folder buttonand select Macintosh HD (or rather the name of your hard disk) from the pop up menu. Select System Folder from the next pop-up menu. In turn, select the Claris folder, then the Claris Stationery folder in exactly the same way. Finally, hit Save.

Notice the name and location of the original report we used as our model is unchanged, but an identical item, called Report Stationery (WP), now appears in the

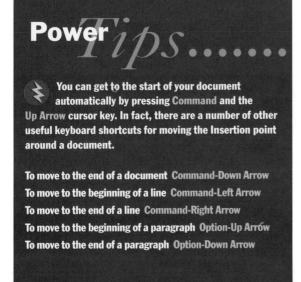

You can then call up your own templates.

pop up Stationery menu.

To use this new template, select New from the pull-down File menu. Pull down the Stationery menu and select Report Stationery. Then click the OK button. The document looks identical to our original but is in fact a new, untitled document. To create a new report, you just edit the untitled document using the techniques you learned earlier in this chapter. When you're happy with it, you can simply Save each new document to the Documents folder.

Power*Tips*........

You can get to the start of your document automatically by pressing Command and the Up Arrow cursor key. In fact, there are a number of other useful keyboard shortcuts for moving the Insertion point around a document.

To move to the end of a document **Command-Down Arrow**

To move to the beginning of a line **Command-Left Arrow**

To move to the end of a line **Command-Right Arrow**

To move to the beginning of a paragraph **Option-Up Arrow**

To move to the end of a paragraph **Option-Down Arrow**

Create Stationery

Now you have seen how labour-saving templates can be, you can become even more productive by customizing the Stationery laid on by Claris to suit your own exacting requirements.

To customize the template provided by *ClarisWorks* for creating memos, for example, choose New from the pull down File menu and select Internal Memorandum from the pull down Stationery menu. Click OK and *ClarisWorks* offers up the Internal Memorandum.

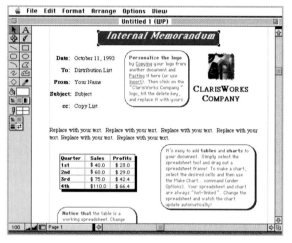

The whole idea of word processing is to give you flexibility.

Power Tips......

⚡ You will soon get used to selecting and deselecting text while editing, but it is worth bearing in mind one shortcut that enables even the fingers and thumbs brigade to quickly and accurately select an appropriate word, line or sentence, just by clicking.

Click twice once on any word and it will be selected, click three times and the line will be selected and click four times to select an entire sentence. You will be amazed at how much effort this simple trick saves you in your journey through Mac life.

⚡ The Scrapbook is a good place to save your own frequently used logos and graphics. You can paste them in and copy them out of Scrapbook with ease.

Looks lousy doesn't it?

The first and most obvious improvement that can be made is to replace the somewhat austere and dowdy looking logo with an altogether funkier number you will find in the Mac's Scrapbook. You can also create your own logos – using *ClarisWorks*' drawing and painting tools as explained in Chapter 7 – and paste them into the memo in the same way.

Open the Scrapbook by selecting Scrapbook from the pull down Apple Menu.

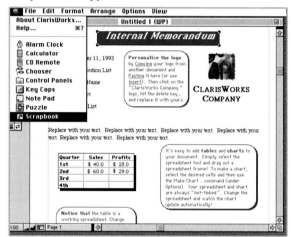

Remember that your whole Mac is integrated as one unit...

Click on the scroll bar at the bottom of the Scrapbook window to scroll through the available selections. When you get to the memo logo, click to select it and choose Copy from the pull down Edit menu.

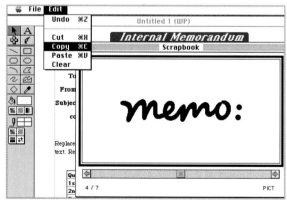

You can cut and paste from the Mac's Scrapbook utility.

(Notice the *ClarisWorks* menu bar has been replaced by the very simple Scrapbook menu bar because Scrapbook is the currently active application.) Now close the Scrapbook, by clicking the little square at the top left hand corner of the Scrapbook window. The logo has been saved to the Mac's internal Clipboard.

You should now find yourself back in the memo stationery document. Click the logo 'Internal Memorandum' to select it and hit delete.

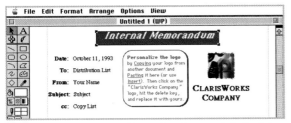

The use of even simple graphics makes documents look slick.

The logo appears to have vanished, but there is one further thing to do before you paste in your own logo.

Logos for example are a great way to create an impression.

Click on the Text tool (the box with the letter A) in the tool palette to the left of the document window. (You will learn more about *ClarisWorks*' tools palettes in future chapters.)

Change things around in order to get just the right feel.

Drag the I-beam across the empty space where the logo was and behold you see a highlighted text field. This is the 'Internal Memorandum' text field; in other words the text part of the logo you last saw superimposed over the logo's gray background. You can't see it at the moment because the text is white on a (now) white background. Hit delete again and it's gone.

Why not make the whole thing look a little friendlier?

Now select Paste from the pull down File menu or press Command-V, and your new funkier Memo logo appears, justified to the left of the document window.

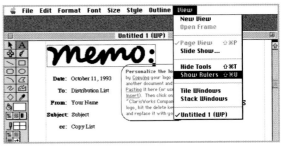

But make sure that everything lines up correctly...

Select the logo (and choose Show Rulers from the pull down View menu, if you can't see the horizontal ruler showing).

...because friendly is not a synonym for sloppy, after all!

Center the logo by hitting the Center alignment button. You can now tidy up your new template by selecting and deleting frames as you see fit.

The spreadsheet frame, for example (the small table lower down the document), will probably be surplus to requirements in the majority of memos, so delete it. The same goes for the huge paint frame lower down. It's easy to add them again later if you feel you can't live without them.

HOW TO Paint

This is probably as good a point as any to introduce the *ClarisWorks* Tools palette, that esoteric-looking collection of brushes and stuff over to the left of your document window. If you don't see the tools palette, select Show Tools from the pull down View menu.

These tools are a unique feature of integrated programs or 'Works packages' in that they allow you to use the same palette of tools in a number of different application environments. You can, for example, create a paint frame in a word-processing document and paint as though you were in a drawing or paint document. Similarly you can build spreadsheets and charts into page layout documents and text frames into drawing documents. These tools are not common to generic word-processing packages. That is why they are being covered right at the end of this chapter.

In this simple example we will add a green 2pt rule to our logo and generate some graffiti in a small paint frame just to demonstrate the principle. If you want to learn how to create a more professional effect, turn to the next chapter.

The Line tool.

To create the rule, select the Line tool from the tools palette. Click where you want the line to start, drag the line, and release the mouse button where you want to finish. If you want the rule to snap automatically to the vertical or horizontal grids, or to 45°, press Shift while you drag.

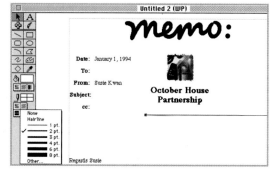

Drawing straight lines gives that modernist, clean feel.

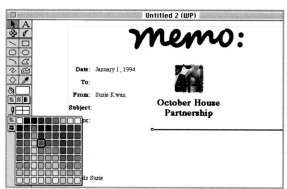

If you've got a color printer, why not make the most of it?

You can also specify the color of the (selected) line by clicking the Pen Color tool menu (a color palette will appear) and placing the cursor over the color you decide that you like best.

The next thing to do is to design a rough logo, just to get you used to the idea of working with frames.

To get rid of the *ClarisWorks* logo first, click to select it and press delete. Then select the Paint tool from the tool palette. In the document the Paint tool becomes a paintbrush icon that you use to drag out a paint frame. Once the frame is drawn you will see that the brush is transformed into a pencil and an extended palette of tools becomes available to you. Use the pencil to draw a logo. Then select the Spray Can from the extended palette, choose a color by clicking on the lower paint bucket icon and placing the cursor the color you want, and spray away.

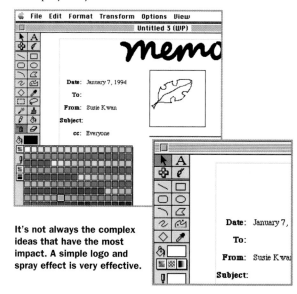

It's not always the complex ideas that have the most impact. A simple logo and spray effect is very effective.

62

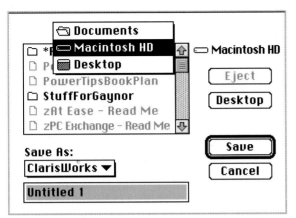

We can't reinforce this too much: make sure to save work.

Select Save As from the File menu and use the skills you painfully acquired earlier on to navigate your way to the Stationery folder. You will find it inside the Claris folder, in the System folder on your Mac's hard disk. Type in the name of the file which in this case is Internal Memorandum, and make sure you select Stationery from the Save As menu. Once you're in the right place, Stationery, hit Save.

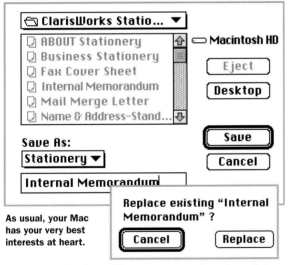

As usual, your Mac has your very best interests at heart.

Your Mac will ask you if you want to replace the existing file Internal Memorandum. Hit Replace. Now every time you select Internal Memorandum from the Stationery your personalised template will appear.

The other word processing templates in *ClarisWorks'* Stationery menu can be personalised in the same way, renamed or deleted, if you feel inclined, by clicking your way to the Stationery folder and dragging unwanted templates into the trash.

To rename Stationery files, double click your way from the hard disk icon, through the System folder and the Claris folder until you see a line up similar to the one shown below.

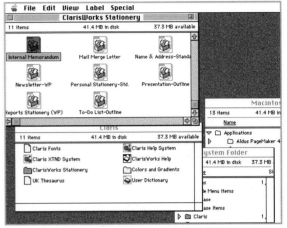

You don't have to be stuck with a huge, long-winded name.

Select the file name you want to change just as you would any other piece of text, and once it is highlighted type over it in the same way. If you want to delete a file, click once on it and drag it to the Trash.

HOW TO Mail Merge

One last trick you may find useful when working with simple letters and documents is the mail merge facility. Mail merging is a very powerful technique for sorting large numbers of names and addresses from a database and of superimposing them automatically into the address fields of company letterheads and faxes – ideal for doing mass mail-outs to clients, friends, the combined heads of state of the G7 group of countries and your inestimable fan club. The one drawback is you have to lick the envelopes yourself.

First you have to have a *ClarisWorks* contacts database (turn to Chapter 9 to find out how to set one up). If you do have a database, and you have a document you'd like to send to selected members of it, the next thing you probably want to learn is how to merge the two. The first step is to set up the merge document – that is, the document you want to send – and to specify the field variables that tell *ClarisWorks* where the database fields are to be inserted. Those are the names and addresses.

Prepare to Merge

Field variables can be attached to any *ClarisWorks* document that incorporates a text frame. A pure word processing document is effectively a single extended text frame, so we can place field variables anywhere we so wish.

Let's say we want to send out a party invitation to a number of friends. We need to create a text document, add a graphic perhaps or a piece of clip art, append a salutation at the head of each printed page, and to print a few labels as well. In this example the graphic was again imported from the Mac's Scrapbook but could just as easily have been created in *ClarisWorks* and imported in the same way.

You should, by now, be able to easily create the basis of your document. Alternatively it is just as good an idea to select Mail Merge stationery from the Stationery Menu and customize it, as it contains pre-defined field variables.

Here's one we created earlier so we'll have to set up the fields ourselves.

So you thought WP was a big bore?

First open your database document by double clicking its icon and select Browse from the pull down Layout menu to check you're inviting the right people.

First Name	Second Name	Address
Victor	Pectoral	Steroid Belt
Mr	Muscle	Northern Wastes
Peter	Spartan	Sparta
Maureen	Visigoth	Central Europe
Samson	n/a	c/o Delilah
Alias	Smith	West Coast, US
Joanne	Hurley	Southampton UK
Christine	Coirot	Orleans, France
Marco	Crisari	Naples, Italy
Julian	Torregiani	Blackheath, UK
Karen	Harvey	Highgate, UK
Alison	Hjul	Belsize Park, UK

Then go back to your merge document, pull down the File menu and select Mail Merge. The Select Data dialog box will appear. This offers you a selection of all currently opened databases. Select Best Friends Database and click OK. The next thing you see should be the Mail Merge palette.

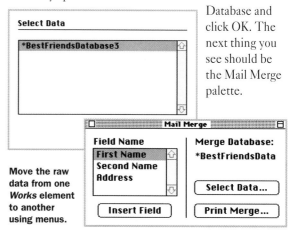

Move the raw data from one *Works* element to another using menus.

From here on, you will be working with your Mail Merge and Database documents in parallel. Click on the fields you want to insert in your document in the Mail Merge palette. A corresponding field in the Mail Merge document will appear at the current insertion point, complete with field delimiters (those two angular quote marks either side of the field name: << >>).

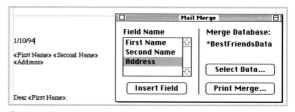

Once you've got the principles, mail merging is really easy.

To insert a first name, for example, click on your word processing document after the word Dear to set the insertion point. Return to the Mail Merge palette and highlight First. The options available to you here are dependent on the database you created in the first place. Then hit Insert Field. The fields will appear in its respective positions in the merge document.

You can also type in field variables manually, generating the field delimiters by pressing Option-Backslash.

If you want the salutation (the first name) to appear in a specific format, **Bold** or *Italicized*, for example, simply highlight the field and embolden or italicize it in the usual way by choosing from the Font, Format and Style Menus.

Words and Pictures
It's a paste-up

7

Owning a Mac doesn't make you a designer or a typographer. But anyone *can* layout a page, or a poster, or a newsletter on a Mac and, as long as you follow some basic rules, it will look good. Programs like *ClarisWorks* – and to some extent word processors like Microsoft *Word* or *WordPerfect* – can do many of the jobs of specialist layout programs, while *PageMaker* and its rival, *XPress*, continue to provide hugely powerful professional tools for page design and makeup, and have become more user friendly. The net result is that combining text and graphics to add power to newsletters, flyers, catalogues, etc. has never been easier.

The elements are likely to include graphics. These may be pictures you've created in a paint program; or computer-generated objects – an illustration using a drawing package, for example. Graphics could also have been scanned in – photographs are often input this way. Or your graphic could perhaps be an image from a CD – either clip art, or your own pictures put onto CD using Kodak's Photo CD, or something similar.

You'll add this to the main text – often known as body copy – which you will have decided to display in a certain style and size using a selected font. You may also want to include some display text – that is headlines, perhaps a caption, or a pull quote taken from the text.

Finally, you may have other page elements – boxes, lines, arrows – to drop into your page.

"We androids dream in full color, but not of sheep"

Be bold in your design.

Preparation is all

That's it. It's not a difficult job, but it makes sense to plan your work first. Everything will go more smoothly if you finish each constituent part of your layout before you begin the process of assembly. There's another reason to plan. Text is easier to edit when it's in a word

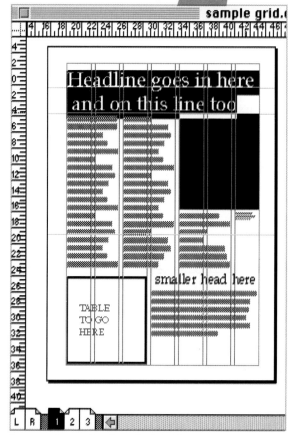

A page under construction – the faded lines represent text (this is called greeking). The blue lines are grid lines

processing package. Likewise graphics, which may be less editable in the form they arrive on your document than in their original state. (See graphics formats later in the chapter.)

Finally, be sure you know what is going to happen to your layout once it's finished. This will have a bearing on which type of fonts you use, on the type of graphics you could include, the colours you should pick – or not pick. Is your work destined for a laser printer, and some hand collating, a colour printer off-site, or a fully fledged graphics bureau – and, in which case, is it going to be produced as film, or bromide? (See 'preparing for bureaux' later in this chapter.)

As a rule of thumb, if you're producing your work on a printer you know, make sure you don't mix fonts – use either PostScript or TrueType (some TrueType fonts came with your Mac). If your work is going further, it makes sense to use PostScript fonts which are the reprographics industry standard. You need to make sure your bureau holds the fonts you've used – don't send them yours, because that's violating the copyright.

On the graphics side, if you're using a bureau ask them what formats they'll need to process your work. If you're using different programs check which formats they will take before starting work.

In this chapter we're using *ClarisWorks* and occasionally *PageMaker* to explain how to put pictures and text together to produce different types of projects. *PageMaker* is a specialist DTP program, *ClarisWorks* a humble do-it-all. Like all Mac applications, though, they use many of the same tools (although at different levels of precision). You can apply many of the effects explained here to both applications, and many more.

HOW TO Drop in a Picture

If you just want to drop pictures into text, you can do that. In fact, it's possible, simple and surprisingly effective to add logos, or headers, or in-line graphics, to produce business documents, letters, or simple news reports.

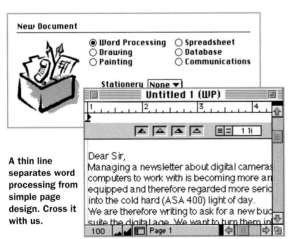

A thin line separates word processing from simple page design. Cross it with us.

Here we're adding a header and a picture to a *ClarisWorks* document. First open the document in Word Processing. Here we've set the page up as an A4 document. Choose a type style from the Style menu and type in the text you need for your document.

You will need to use the Zoom effects for accurate graphics.

If you want more space you can kill the Tool palette at the side of the screen by clicking on the small square at the top left of the window. To get it back do the reverse. You can add pictures to text in *ClarisWorks* in one of two ways. They can either be placed so that they are a part of the text – in which case, they are in-line graphics, or they can be dropped in to the document so that they are independent of the text you already have.

In-line graphics

Place an image from here.

In-line graphics are not very manipulable, but they will stay where you put them in relation to your text – even if you cut it to ribbons. First make sure your I-beam is flashing where you want the graphic to land, then choose Insert under the File menu. Choose your image by cycling through your different folders. And hit Return.

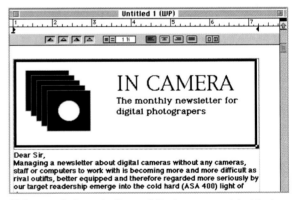

Make sure that you don't crunch the images up against text.

You can resize your image by selecting it, grabbing the corners and pulling. Notice that it won't go beyond the confines of the text boundaries – if you hold it by the corner you can resize it in proportion. If you do distort the graphic discard it and reinsert.

You can paste an image in-line using the Cut or Copy and Paste routine (see Chapter 6) too, using virtually the same process.

Independent graphics

Independent graphics do what they say; they can float clear of boundaries set up by the document.

Here we introduced columns to the document. We chose a two-column grid.

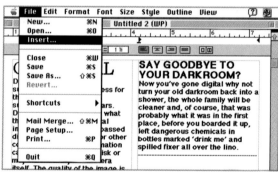

Using columns makes for easier reading. But what about the pix?

To place an independent graphic on a *ClarisWorks* document, make sure your text is not selected – hit the Arrow tool on the side bar to make sure.

Don't worry, you can cross column lines with the right graphic.

Then go to the same menu and choose Insert, or use cut and paste. The result is a free-floating graphic. You can pick it up, move it, and resize it beyond text boundaries such as columns. Cut and pasted images can also be independent.

The illustration on the left is an in-line graphic, while the illustration on the right floats free. The difference is clear.

Text Wraps

You do actually want your graphic object to have some bearing on how text behaves, since the point is to combine them. Independent objects can have text wraps applied to them. Text wraps determine the basic relationship between the graphic object and the text. They dictate whether the text runs around the object runs over it, or, in some cases, jumps across it.

Notice the camera logo is simply sitting on top of the text in the picture. This is because no text wrap has been applied to it. To apply a text wrap, select your object – use the arrow tool and then click on it once. Go to Options, and check Text Wrap.

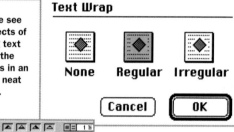

Here we see the effects of running text around the graphics in an orderly, neat fashion.

You'll face a dialog box offering three self-explanatory options.

Applying a wrap to the camera logo means that text curls itself around the camera. Wherever you move this graphic (select it, pick up, and drag) the text will rearrange itself around it. Choose the irregular wrap if the shape that needs wrapping is complex or the text will wrap itself around the object's bounding box, not the object itself. You may need to do some fine tuning of the text if the wrap results in some strange word breaks. You can wrap across columns too.

Soft returns allow you to start a new line in the middle of a paragraph so you can arrange text in a way that makes sense – after you have inserted a text wrap or whenever it's needed. To make a soft line break hit return while holding down the shift key on your keyboard. You can also use this to avoid awkward sense splits – for example, first and second names on two lines. Remember, however, if used in excess it will mean gaps in your text.

67

Words and Pictures

If you want to insert a letterhead across a page with columns place it as an independent graphic and apply a text wrap to the letterhead after you've imported it. That way your text won't disappear under the letterhead at the top of each column – and your letterhead won't try and compress itself into a single column either.

Who's On Top?

An inserted graphic lands on top of your text. It doesn't have to be there, it could sit behind. Like all other graphics applications *ClarisWorks* has a system of layers – imagine them like tracing paper. Selecting the camera

and sending it to the back using the Arrange command under Options leaves the text free to run all over the front of the image (make sure it doesn't have a text wrap on or this won't work).

Graphic Reservations

If you can't find the image you want when you go to Insert, it may be in a format that *ClarisWorks* can't recognize. That's because there are various graphics formats, and what *ClarisWorks* can't read, it won't let you see. Try opening the document and closing it in a different format. (See Chapter 8 on paint and drawing.)

68

HOME GROWN
There's another way to get simple graphics into your word processed document in *ClarisWorks.* That is to draw them straight in using the drawing tools at the left-hand side. Click the Arrow tool, select a tool in the graphics palette – always open in the word processing section of Works – draw your shape, and apply an irregular text

wrap. This example used a disc, filled with yellow using the paint bucket. The black outline around the yellow disk was discarded in favour of yellow from the pen palette. Then we added a smaller disc, filled it with black, grouped them under the Arrange menu and copied them. Voilà. Record sales.

secret or confidential, or to group documents in a single project. You can also simply use it as a graphic effect. Try using different tiles and tints with the paint bucket tool for effect.

IT WAS YOUR IDEA
Remember not to delete if you select an object and then change your mind about choosing it – you selected it, so that's what will be deleted. It's very easy to do, but you feel stupid afterwards.

RETIRE GRACEFULLY
If you place an image and things go badly wrong retire gracefully, delete the whole image and replace or insert it. It's easier than trying to de-distort a picture of your beloved which now resembles Spock without the ears. When you Insert an image, your original document remains untouched.

USING LAYERS
Text is transparent to graphics. This means it's possible to run a graphic behind text – this is called a ghost or stamp. You can use this to mark papers as being

HOW TO Jazz it up

Make Drop Caps

The Frames technology in *ClarisWorks* means you can access different tools within other parts of the application as floating frames within a single document.

You can even select a new text frame, within the word processing application. To do this, hold down the Option key while you hit the Text tool (the A) in the side bar. You've opened a text box within your word processor. This has definite uses when working with words you want to treat as objects.

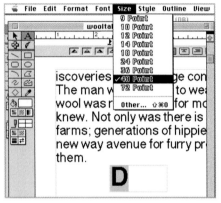

Create your drop cap as a separate item from the text. You can even use a different typeface for added effect.

Option A-tool gives you a new text box. Type in your drop cap. We used D, at 40pt, in bold. Remember you need to select your text, not the handles on the text box, to edit your choice.

Make sure the box is selected. Then choose Regular for the text wrap under the Options menu.

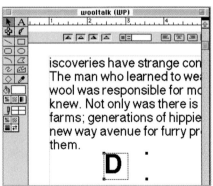

Make sure to give some runaround, but not acres. The correct runaround is really up to your eye for a good design.

Select your text again and drag the box around the letter until it fits snugly. Drag it to the right place – so it lines up with the body text. If you want to be flash you could add a simple coloured box behind the letter. Or select

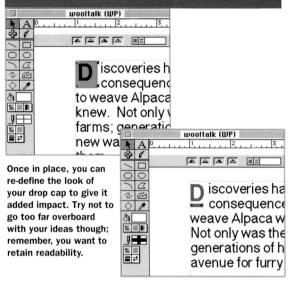

Once in place, you can re-define the look of your drop cap to give it added impact. Try not to go too far overboard with your ideas though; remember, you want to retain readability.

the letter and choose a different coloured text (from text colour under Style, not in the tool bar on the left). You could also emphasise the drop cap with a solid bar below it – use a thick line from the pen palette.

There's more to drop caps than single letters. You can create very useful markers and signposts with this technique.

Use the same process to produce quick vertical headlines. Type in your text, stylise as required, then manipulate the box size for a speedy vertical headline – in this case select-drag by the corners and pull into a long thin shape to run down the side of the text.

If you want headlines that run up the side of the page, you can do that too.

Make a type box with Option and the text tool. Type in your text, sort out a style, then select the box, rather than the text itself. Under Arrange you'll see a rotate tool. Then drag your text where you want it to be placed. Put a text wrap on it under Options. and you're finished.

HOW TO Set up a Newsletter

Using Linked Text

There's a lot you can do with words and pictures to add some zing to a document. But beyond a certain point you'll need more flexibility with text. To produce relatively complex documents – or very irregular ones – you need better text management than a word processor can offer; and perhaps more variety in document size. Enter, somewhat peculiarly, the drawing section of *ClarisWorks* – the most flexible part of works.

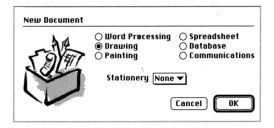

This is very close to the standard way of dealing with text in *XPress* and *PageMaker* – so if you want to graduate you'll understand the metaphor of linked text boxes. Here's how to build a newsletter using linked text.

First, make sure all the pieces you need are assembled, including text and any graphics you want in the layout. Open *ClarisWorks* and choose Drawing. Make sure you turn the Rulers on under Format – use centimetres if you want more precision than inches will provide. Think about the size of the page – check the margins if necessary too.

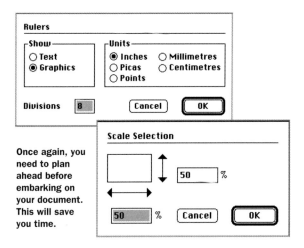

Once again, you need to plan ahead before embarking on your document. This will save you time.

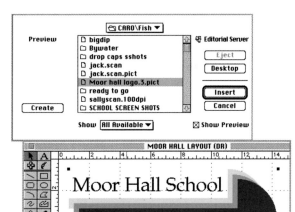

Inserting graphics once again, will add to the look of your work.

First insert your heading or logo if you have one. Here the Moor Hall logo inserted is too large. Select it and use the Scale Selection tool under the Options menu to resize it.

Now it's time to set up linked text boxes. First check Frame Links under the Options menu – if it's on, it's ticked. This means the text frames you are setting up have a relation to each other – and so will the text when you import it (if you can't see this menu, you may be in another *ClarisWorks* mode – if so, skip out of it).

Hit the Text tool on the side bar, then go back into the document and drag out your I-beam to the size of the text box you want (don't worry if you're not sure exactly what size this is, you can fix it later).

You can see a text box with six indicators. Four at the corners are for resizing your box. The one at the top shows that this is the first of a series (once you've set them up) of linked frames. The one at the bottom tells you that you can continue to drag out boxes and text will flow into them in a related way. *Claris* calls this the Continue indicator (if you can't see this, click outside the frame, then click inside once to reselect it).

Set up your text boxes so the word flow is easy to follow.

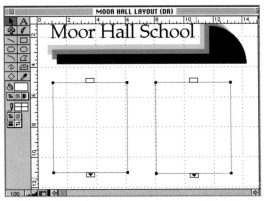

The space between text boxes (gutter) needs fine judgement.

Draw another text box in exactly the same way next to the first. To check their sizes select both frames by shift-selecting – click on one frame, hold down the shift key and click on the next: it should look like the picture above. Use the ruler to line up boxes – there's a thin line on the margin rule which corresponds with the position of your cursor.

Inserting the text is easy. Click on the A tool, click inside the first text box once. Hit Insert – under the File menu – and choose your file. Easy-ish. The text will flow across the text boxes. Make sure the text icon is showing – the boxes are grey lines without the Links protuberances – or you may not see the text files.

If the text is too long for the boxes you have designed

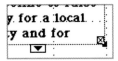

Beware text overflow.

for it small, a crossed box shows at the bottom of the text box. This shows up even when the box is not highlighted, so it's difficult to ignore text with nowhere to go.

If you want to add headlines, draw new text boxes, but check the Link Frames off this time and keep them independent of each other. Drag them across to their position above the text.

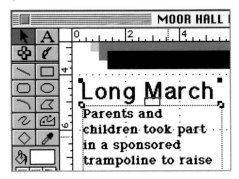

You don't want to link headlines with normal text boxes.

Insert some pictures. Remember, if you want them to flow with the text select within it. If you don't, make sure you haven't by clicking the Arrow draw tool.

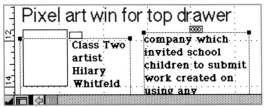

Aligning the edges of the boxes gives that organised look.

To tidy things up you could select the top of your headline box on the left and the text box on the right and choose Arrange. Align the two columns along the bottom line of text.

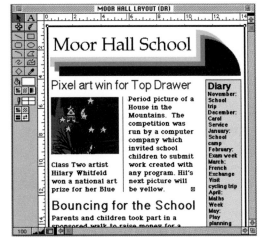

You're ready to print. These principles will serve you well.

Save and print. If you want to use the same basic plan over again, you could save the document under a different name, and delete the text from the boxes. Save the result as a template and use it again. To speed this up, go to the Text tool, choose Command A for select all (this will select the whole of a highlighted text, rather than only what you can see). Then delete. Make sure you do this with highlighted text not boxes, or you'll delete your template.

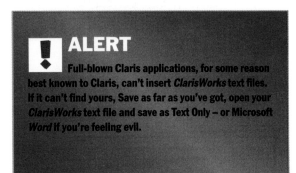

ALERT

Full-blown Claris applications, for some reason best known to Claris, can't insert *ClarisWorks* text files. If it can't find yours, Save as far as you've got, open your *ClarisWorks* text file and save as Text Only – or Microsoft *Word* if you're feeling evil.

HOW TO Set up a Publication

If the work you are doing is a single page, you can probably pick fonts at random, and sort out a style as you go. If you are attempting anything longer, or if you want to set up a template for a regular publication – for example, a newsletter, bulletin, or monthly report – then it's wise to establish styles.

These should include the size of the page, the grid (that is, the arrangements of columns), and also a set of styles for different components of the publication – headlines, body copy, captions for pictures and perhaps pull quotes.

This workthru' explains how to set up custom styles in *ClarisWorks*. In *PageMaker* and *XPress* it is possible to set up an extensive tear-off style palette. The drawing module of *ClarisWorks* gives you a flexible grid, but working with columns in the word processing section provides a fast way to set up a framework for your document. Open a *ClarisWorks* word processing document.

The first decision is the number of columns.

Choose Columns under the Format menu.

72

Once again you will need to plan ahead. Don't be too afraid to experiment at this stage.

We want variable width columns and the dialog box allows specifications for each column to be set. Editing a column grid is simple. Either go back to the Columns box and change the specifications, or use the tools at the top of the page. These either add or take away a column per click – but they will also destroy any irregular columns you've set up. We've will add some text by Inserting so we can see what the page will look like. You may find it easier to type your copy in a separate document and insert it. It's also a useful back up if you delete while adjusting your layout.

Next we need to define some styles. Fish Watch needs body copy. We chose Helvetica. Go to Define Styles under the Style menu. Choose a name, a size, a font and a colour, and give it a name that is easily recognisable. Click Add. Your style will appear in the box above. Click Done. Your style will appear under the Style menu.

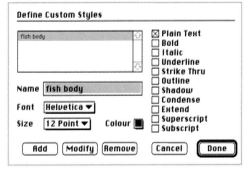

Defining Style Sheets will save you a lot of time in future.

Fish also needs a headline style. We chose Helvetica again, but this time larger and in blue. You can also add a caption face and a pull quote, setting type attributes like Bold as well as colour and size. Remember to click Add each time.

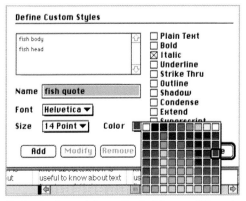

Try to plan for each type of text style you will be using.

The net result is a series of styles under Options.

Because *ClarisWorks* provides shortcuts with these styles, you don't need to pull-down the menu to reach them each time. It's possible to define styles in the same way if you start with a drawing document too.

Applying text styles is a simple act.

It also makes sense to control other text specifications The Paragraph controls under the Format menu allow for the first line of a paragraph to be indented. This can also be done with the ruler. Below the arrow at the left-hand side of the ruler is a small bar; this is the first line indent marker. You can drag it in and every first line will be indented.

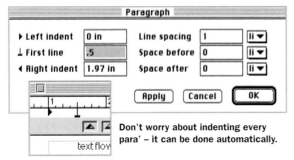

Don't worry about indenting every para' – it can be done automatically.

You can use the same dialog box to set up different leading for text. Leading is the space between lines of text. (The name comes from hot metal printing when slugs of lead were put between the lines when composing text). These controls can be very basic, using lines, or very precise point sizes. You can experiment with different types of leading using point sizes; if you're using 9pt, try 9 on 10pt or 9 on 9.5pt.

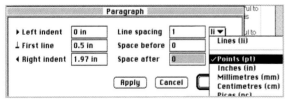

The space between lines (leading) can help or hinder reading.

Once you've got the basic style, you can add the furniture – for example, the heading, and possibly boxes which will be the same each time. Here we've added a Shark Watch logo – for shark sightings.

Once the basic structure is set up, you can add the frills.

You can also add boxes to a template so they'll be ready each time you need to use them. Use Options and then click the Text tool. This gives us a new (and independent) text frame within the one we have. Drag it out across a couple of columns. Type in the box heading – in this case, Dolphin Count. Go to the Line tool and choose 2pt for a line. Drag it across the top of the text (stay within the new text box). Drag a box around it. Then select the box and send it to the back. Adjust the title text within the box. Finally, select the box and add a wrap. Group the objects – under the Arrange menu – to hold them together. Each time the publication is opened the box will be waiting to be filled.

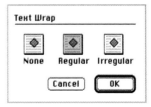

Plan for the future once again.

You can set page numbers so that they are in the right place each time, and set up styles for these.

Finally, save your work as stationery, and you have a template for a newsletter. To do that go to Save and choose the Stationery option. Each time you open you will start from the same basis. You can save drawing documents as stationery too, if you want to use the drawing document as a basis for your work.

A Word About Text

If you are starting a newsletter from scratch and you intend to insert different blocks of text, it makes sense to save them in different files. You may also find it's better not to format in advance. Inset paragraphs, for example, may simply have to be taken out again and reset for the layout page.

A Point About Points

Points are a printer's measure of type and give a precise way of measuring the size of type and of setting leading. Body copy in newspapers would be around 9pt. Leaded copy is defined by two point sizes: (font size and leading size). This means that a paragraph of 9pt (text) on 9pt (leading) would be tighter than 9 on 12pt.

How to Source Graphics

There are three ways to source graphics for your documents. The first is to create them yourself, either in a Works package or in a drawing or painting package like *Illustrator*, *FreeHand*, *Painter* or even *Kid Pix*. (see Chapter 8.)

73

The second is to scan them in either using your own scanner or by going to a repro house to do this. To do this you need to know some basic scanning rules. These apply whatever the application you are using: the point is to ensure that the resolution of the image you are scanning is correct and that it is in a usable format.

Scanning Rules

You don't need to scan at the maximum resolution of your scanner. This wastes valuable storage space and won't necessarily give you better results because the quality of the image depends on how it is printed and on the size it is used at.

Line screens are the way a program like *PageMaker* or *XPress* treats a graphic image. You output images at a certain number of lines per inch. 133lpi is common for colour work. As a rule of thumb, when you scan in greyscale or colour you should scan at 2.5 times the line screen that will be used when the image is sent to film or bromide. If your work is going to be used for output to a colour or greyscale or black and white laser printer, scan at its resolution.

If you are scanning an image for an on-screen presentation there's no point scanning at more than 72dpi because that's the resolution of the Mac screen.

Remember:

1. Scanning big, and then reducing, improves quality.
2. If you intend to blow up the image you should take this into account. If you double the image size, double the resolution.

A third way to source images is to use Photo CD – assuming you have access to a CD-ROM player. Photo CD allows you to take ordinary film you've used in any camera to a processing house where the images will be put onto a Photo CD. From there you can place them in documents. Photo CD has the advantage that somebody else (the processing agent) has invested in a very expensive scanner, and users benefit from the results this produces.

To use a Photo CD, insert it into a CD-ROM drive (to make sure it's there, find the icon on the desktop – it should appear a few seconds after you add the disc to the drive), then choose Insert. By moving back to the desktop you should be able to choose your image in the normal way.

Power *Tips*..........

I COMMAND YOU: if you lose boxes try Select All (Command A). It will show you where everything is. Don't hit delete at this point or you'll lose everything selected – which is every thing. To copy styles between different documents you can copy the ruler, using Command-Shift-C and Command-Shift-V.

DESIGN TIPS: USE capitals for the opening word of an article. This is useful on a complicated page because it draws the eye to the opening. Some newspapers use a bold first paragraph for this effect.

BULLET POINTS: Option 8 gives you a decent bullet point. • Like so. You can scale it to fit with your text. The bullet point can either be "full out" – that is, against the edge of the page – or indented. A better alternative may be to use Zapf Dingbats.

TO SCAN OR NOT TO SCAN: don't be ruggedly individual for the sake of it. A good scan could make all the difference to the final quality of your work. If you've got the equipment to produce good quality pages, but no color scanner, and you're going to use an imagesetter to output your work, at least consider asking a bureau to do you a scan.

ONE TWO MANY SPACES: don't add two spaces after a period or full-point. Digital type (fonts) uses proportional spacing that allocates space as it's needed – for example, a W takes up more space than an I. If you add an extra space it will tend to look wrong because the font has already provided the right spacing.

You can set up a paragraph with only the first line pulled out, by holding down the Option key before dragging the first line marker where you want it to go.

Power *Graphics* ....

WHITE ON BLACK

Here is a simple and elegant solution to the 'dowdy text' syndrome occasionally suffered by people who only have black and white output facilities (and most people don't have professional outputting facilities at their beck and call). White On Black or White Out-of Black is known in the trade as a WOB – for obvious reasons.

It is a very useful effect for box headings or main banner headlines – if you're prepared to use up a great deal of black ink – and you don't have to have a money-mountain to output Wobbed text.

Wobs are simple to produce in almost any program. Here we used *PageMaker* but you can do it in *ClarisWorks*. Remember to sort yourself out an independent text box first (Options, then the A tool) – that way you can place the text in the middle of the box more precisely.

Type your heading. Choose a style and apply it using the Size and Style menu. Draw a box and fill it with solid black. Try and make it roughly the right size. Highlight your text. Choose no color.

The text will disappear but you can still select the text box with the pointer tool. Find it and drag it onto the black box. Align the two boxes to centre your text. (Use the Align commands under Options if you're working in *ClarisWorks*; in any case remember to shift-select to select two things at once.) Select the box, hold down the shift key and select the text too.

When you're happy you could group the elements and lock them to stop them drifting out of place and make it simple to move them around. Again select both and then use Group under the Align menu.

If you can't find the text when you drag it over the box, you've probably got the actions in the wrong order. Select the box and use the Send to Back command. under Options.

If you want to get smart use half white on black. If you want to be silly and get caught out, use a Wob for a box-out that people have to reply to; for example a competition or reader reply card to your local newsletter.

Why is this a silly idea? How many people do you know who use white pens to write with?

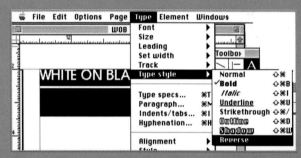

The use of White Out of Black (Wob) text is very popular in newspaper design where only black and white print outputting is available. Here we have illustrated a number of ways in which you can use Wobs to liven up documents that you are going to print out from your home printer. Once again, a very, very basic principle used with imagination can produce some eye-catching effects for you.

HOW TO Create a Page

Which ever application you use, designing a publication requires careful thought and attention to detail. Set up your templates, sort out a style sheet and stick to basic guidelines and you won't go wrong.

This page, the first in a regular newsletter, points out some of the dos – and don'ts.

Smart Quotes: Always use typeset quotes. These are curly quotes rather than the straight kind. They blend better with typefaces and look more professional. ClarisWorks includes a smart quotes option. To set this find Preferences under the Edit menu: choose Text from the left-hand side (click on it with your mouse), and check the smart quotes box on the right.

If you import files which don't have smart quotes you can apply them using one of four key combinations:

Option-[gives you "
Option-Shift-[gives you "
Option-] gives you '
Option-Shift-] gives you '

Font warning! Don't use too many fonts in document. It will look distracting and will have no cohesion. Stick to two or three faces. Consider using variants of the same face for contrast – for example, a bold or italic version of the basic body copy for the headline.

Space: let your work breathe. As a general rule give headlines in large text enough space to work, while keeping body copy fairly tight to make reading it simple.

Keylines: if the image you are using fades away, you need to add a keyline to harden the edge and provide clarity. To do this either use the line tool or put a black box behind the picture. The control on this is less precise but it does make sure you won't have a space between the picture and the frame. To add a keyline in this way with *ClarisWorks*, draw a square, using the square tool, and fill it using the fill tool or paintbucket (to change the colour double click and use black). Then select this square and move it over your image. Keep it selected, choose Options from the menu and then Send to the back. Use rules and lines to anchor the page.

There is little point in just talking about a document; what's called for here is a practical example of some basic principles. Here we have a test page comprising some of the most common elements of good newsletter design and layout. We've used very few graphics, very few fancified typefaces or fonts.

We've also tried to pack in as much text as possible in order to convey information – paper is not cheap – without making the whole thing look like a tedious textbook. So how did we do it? What tips could you make use of? We reveal all in the following Master Class – which comes complete with annotations…

1 Try and make your headlines fit. If not, the top 'deck' is better fuller than the second or third – as in this text headline. It makes sense to run a headline right across the top of your story.

2 Run captions at the side or below a picture. They should draw your readers in. Here the caption style is in Franklin Gothic, as is the body copy, but it has been italicised to lift it out.

3 Break up long stretches of text with crossheads. These can be taken from the text below or could describe what you're writing about – they do draw a reader's eye though.

4 Give your crossheads space to do their job by putting a line space above the head.

5 Try and run different elements on a page. Contents boxes are a good idea because they act as a taster. But a box with short items could fulfil the same function.

6 Drop capitals can add interest and emphasis where a story begins. You could add an in-line graphic to do the same job.

N

D

M

H is Er Be

device outputtin

Using new s process "Fixed g the enti full-colo

Benv surgeon captain.

8 ars in arg Moriarty

Acco state, w

12

well-kno Top Kansas residing Max Wu grasp nurtured lawyers process must be property compan

Mr W I as he manage heavily fe membe former a security,

Com discover damned a purely out on u the back

ews *update*

VOLUME 1

CTOR BENWAY KES HISTORY

nade this week as former
of the Year, Dr Gerald T
unveiled his revolutionary
$2, high-end, five-color

trusty ColorClassic, his
and color-separation
tyleWriter II that he had
t", he was able to output
ts of the *Hite Report* in
oit scans.

s the company's former
eyball and rifle-shooting
een in retirement for some
e stormed into Senior VP
duct Development, Dave
s office last Tuesday.
floriarty: "Benway was in a
s verging on hysteria. He
abbed me by the throat
and screamed, 'You vapid,
viperous, felon, you will
suffer for this the way they
made me and Reich
l' he then shook my hand
nvited me to lunch at a
ar",

nent have been flown to
Benway is known to be
ime. According to CEO,
way's inventive mind and
nology was obviously
Nova Corps. I, and my
erefore, that any n
ge from this aging ge
d also as the intellectual
Corps and its subsidiary
uestion about it",
speaking from NovaFlight
eral highly placed Nova
f sped towards Benway's
mestead. One of the staff
mpanying Mr Wump is
nd now VP in charge of
Sarge – Cassidy.
on the thrilling new
y explained: "Benway is
s exit of the company wa
t. He had no need to walk
ad for some awful part of
here like this. Has he no

New printing techniques could totally
revolutionize the way you work and play.

feelings for his fellow employees? Has he no
gratitude? Has he slipped into the kind of
selfish individualism that has marked out our
modern age as the last stand before the
apocalypse that will engulf and remap the
known universe and all of time? Dammit,
the man is a weenie and we are going to
kick his behind all the way to Anchorage.
Don't quote me on that though… it could
be Montreal of even Baltimore!".

CAPTAIN OF THE TOWN

At the time of going to press, Benway was
unavailable for comment. He is known to
be hunkered down at this time working on
a new project which he claimed in a TV
interview yesterday would: "Let every Mac
in the known and living worlds do without
RAM from now until eternity. That's right
my boys, RAM is a thing of the past".
Your reporter understands that the new
device makes use of revolutionary Orgone
techniques as well as several tons of raw
ish, beef and old-fashioned lead slugs,
previously used in hot metal printing.
We, like the rest of you await
developments with baited breath.

CONTENTS

MAC MADE EASY "RIGHT CHOICE" SAYS Ms BILL LEE

The choice of Champions was just one
of the claims made for Mac Made
Easy, the latest work on the
construction of Scottish ancestries, Apple
Macintosh usage and hamburger ingestion.
At the time of going to press, no one is
entirely certain who this quote can be
attributed to. Nevertheless, 96-year-old Ms
Bill Lee has stepped forward to claim that the
entire project was her idea from the very
beginning.
"Don't make me laugh ol' boy, ol' boy!
This entire, rolling paperchase has been my
conspiracy since word one. No one, and I
mean no one outside of the president himself
has inked a single period, capital letter of
colon aside from my good self. Believe me
when I say that this has been a labour of love
all the goddam way". Ms Lee is known to be
suffering from a severe case of Grandiloquent
Depressive Syndrome following a crushing
defeat in a game of Varsity football where she
QB'd the Nantucket Survivors to a 76-03
defeat against the Cupertino Coolers last Fall
in Wisconsin.
Real-life authors of Mac Made Easy,
Caroline Bassett and Guy Sneesby today
claimed to have no knowledge of Lee, any
works on Scottish ancestry, hamburgers or
the Survivors v Coolers game.
"As far as we are concerned, it is a book
about empowering new Mac users. We've
tried to avoid technospeak, jargon and we've
made sure to use as much color illustration
as we could. That's really", was the only
comment we could extract from the
fabulously famous pair.

1

7 Make sure your columns line up.
You can do this by checking the
baseline alignment. Make sure the
body of your text hits the line at the
bottom of the page otherwise you will
be left with an untidy document.

8 Avoid widows and orphans. These
are short lines or single words left at
the bottom or top of a page – cut or add
a few words of copy to avoid them. If
you don't, they end up by looking like
this.

9 Points can make a point – use
text sizes sensitively.

10 Respect your own grid. You could
run copy across a double column, but
let the basic rules show through. This
will provide consistency and make
your newsletter easier to read.

11 Use reasonable column widths –
neither too narrow to read or too broad
to take in quickly.

12 Watch out for runarounds – if you
place a graphic with a wraparound
check the words around it are still
readable. If not you can use a soft
return to pull them around

13 Just black and white? This is not a
disaster. There's much that can be done
with monochrome and shades of black to
make a document look good – after all
most of the world's press have done it for
hundreds of years! Ideas include radials,
text effects, boxes, white on black etc.

77

Paint works

How to create *designs* *for letterheads business cards and* icons

8

Metal **Fish**

In this chapter we will describe the activities and tricks you need to know in order to create designs for your own logos, letterheads, business cards, greetings cards, labels and even new icons for your desktop. You will also learn how to use a wide variety of drawing and painting tools along the way.

The sample application used in this chapter is, once again *ClarisWorks*, but you will find the tools and techniques apply equally to most Mac drawing and painting packages. To begin with, we will use the Drawing environment in *ClarisWorks* to create a logo for the fictional publishing company called Burning Books. We will then progress to a detailed tutorial on creating low-cost but effective illustrations (such as the one on the left) to brighten up your documents...

ClarisWorks

If you don't already have *ClarisWorks* running, double click on the *ClarisWorks* icon in your Applications folder to launch it.

New Document

○ Word Processing ○ Spreadsheet
● Drawing ○ Database
○ Painting ○ Communications

Stationery [None ▼]

[Cancel] [OK]

File	Edit	Format	A
New...	⌘N		
Open...	⌘O		
Insert...			
Close	⌘W		
Save	⌘S		
Save As...	⇧⌘S		
Revert...			
Shortcuts	▶		
Mail Merge...	⇧⌘M		
Page Setup...			
Print...	⌘P		
Quit	⌘Q		

The New Document dialog box that appears prompts you to select a document type. Click on Drawing and then hit OK. If you are already working in ClarisWorks, you may have to select New from the pull down File menu to bring up the dialog box. Again, click on Drawing and hit OK.

This opens an untitled Drawing document. If the document window is too large, you can resize it by clicking on the tiny icon at the bottom right-hand corner of the window and dragging.

The *ClarisWorks* Drawing environment provides simple tools for creating shapes like rectangles, lines, circles, arcs and polygons, but by combining them you can build up quite sophisticated images.

This is your electronic canvas. The grid lines are optional.

HOW TO Get Started

Start the logo by clicking on the Rectangle tool in the tools palette at the top left-hand side of the document window.

When you move the cursor back to the drawing area, it should now appear as a crosshair.

Click on the grid where you want the drawing to begin and, holding the mouse button down, draw out a rectangle in the shape of a book cover. Release the mouse button and the rectangle stays selected.

That means it is still active (notice the handles at its four corners). You can get rid of it, if you don't like it, by hitting Delete, or you can resize it using any of the four handles. To move a selected object, all you have to do is to click inside it and drag.

You may find that when you move the rectangle, you can't place it exactly where you want it because, just at the last second, it snaps to an invisible grid. You can see some of the dotted lines of the grid criss-crossing the page. To see the full rulers, select Show Rulers from the View menu.

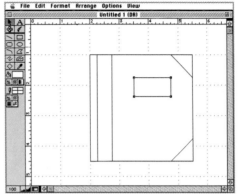

Showing rulers gives you some idea of where you are going.

At this stage the company logo is still looking a little rudimentary, so to embellish it a little, select the Line tool from the tools palette. Draw a couple of diagonal lines and two vertical lines, to represent the leather binding at the corners and the spine of the book. Draw lines by clicking a start point and dragging with the mouse button held down.

Select the Rectangle tool again and pull the cursor diagonally down to the right to draw out a nameplate. Notice that each item is treated as a separate object. Click on the rectangular nameplate and four handles

will appear. When you click on a handle and drag you can change the size and dimensions of an object, although it will always maintain its basic shape.

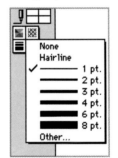

Keep your initial designs simple. You can add to them later.

Alter the thickness of a line by clicking on it and selecting an option from the pen size palette.

The Pen Size tool is located under the small icon of a pen and you open it by clicking on the icon with the three graduated lines. Hold the mouse button down and a palette pops open. Alter the line width by clicking anywhere in this box.

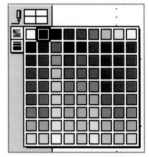

The opening lines are really just guides. Don't get too heavy.

You can also alter a line's colour or add arrowheads, in much the same way. The point to remember is that only the currently selected object takes on the new attributes.

To change the attributes of a group of objects, you have to select the whole group. Go back to the document and draw out a marquee that encompasses the entire logo. That's right, the whole glorious thing. All of a sudden, all the objects have sprouted handles.

Click on the Pen Colour tool and select a colour from the pop-up palette – the selected lines immediately take on that colour. The current pen colour is always displayed in the crosshairs (the pen indicator box) next to the pen icon.

Paint works

Now that the the logo is starting to take shape, it is probably a good time to save what you've done so far. Select Save As from the pull down File menu or press Command-S (the Command button and S together). Type in a file name, make sure the Save As dialog box is set to Documents, and hit Save. This saves your logo to the folder on the hard disk called Documents. Each time you save, this document will be updated.

Once again, remember to save. You'll appreciate this one day.

As you work through the design, remember to save regularly. If your Mac crashes, you will lose all the work

you did since your last save.

To return to a saved document after a break, look for it in the Documents folder and double click on its icon. Alternatively, select Open from the File menu and double click on the document's name in the dialog box that appears.

PowerTips

To select a group of objects quickly, press Command at the same time as you draw the marquee. This type of marquee only has to touch objects to select them. It may not seem much but once you start using the package in anger, you won't do it any other way. To select or deselect a number of individual items in a group, press Shift and click on the objects in turn.

Press Shift as you drag the Line, Arc or Ellipse tools and your lines will automatically snap to 45 or 90 degrees, turning your rectangles into squares, your ellipses to circles and your arcs into pie quarters.

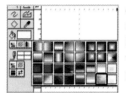

Add Colour

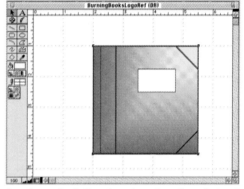

The Gradient palette.

ClarisWorks, in common with most other drawing packages, lets you flesh out your designs with vibrant colours just by pointing and clicking.

Click on the outline of the logo. Look for the four handles to make sure it is selected. Click on the Gradient icon and drag the cursor over one of the fill options in the pop-up Gradient palette.

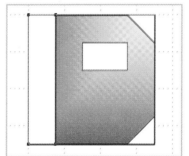

See those simple lines have been transformed at a stroke.

Notice that the whole logo fills up apart from the nameplate. That is because the drawing consists mainly of broken lines. Remember that all objects are treated individually, so the corner triangles, although they look like an enclosed groups, don't stand a chance of resisting the fill. So that we can give the corners their own colour, we will redraw them, using the Polygon tool.

Click on the Polygon icon in the tools palette, and click on each point of the triangle in turn. The sticky dotted line that clings to the cursor like a piece of gum on your shoe disappears when you double click back on the start point. A white triangular object should now appear super-imposed over the graduated background.

You can control the flow of the hues to give more impact.

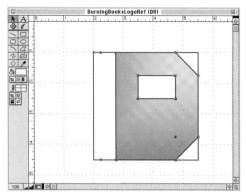

Now thicken up the keylines to give a more solid appearance.

Repeat the procedure until both the corners and the spine are whited out. To maintain a consistent line width of 2pt, select the whole logo with a marquee and choose 2pt from the Pen Size menu.

Change the colour of each polygon in turn by selecting it, clicking on the Colour Fill icon in the tools palette and choose a colour from the pop up colour palette. Repeat the procedure until all the polygons are filled.

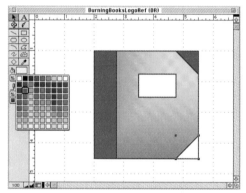

The next thing is to enhance the look of the edges.

These new objects effectively occupy a separate layer floating above the original design. Notice that a line disappeared when we filled the polygon nearest the spine. The line still exists; it is just hidden behind the new polygon. To get it back, click on the polygon and select Move to Back from the Arrange menu. Click on the line and select Move to Front, and then click on the book outline and select Move to Back.

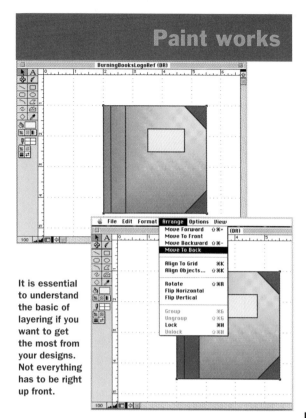

It is essential to understand the basic of layering if you want to get the most from your designs. Not everything has to be right up front.

81

Any object can be selected and rearranged in this way. This is perhaps the key distinction between Drawing and Painting. Painting documents consist of a single layer of coloured dots. You'll find out how this affects the editing environment later on.

Before we are finished with the book, we are going to add a pattern fill to create a texture for the nameplate. Select the nameplate and then click on the Pattern Fill icon in the tools palette. Select an appropriate pattern from the Pattern palette and release the mouse button. You can change the colour of the pattern by selecting the object again and choosing a colour from the Colour Fill palette.

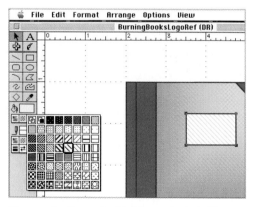

The use of patterns shouldn't be overlooked either.

To add text to the nameplate, click on the Text tool – the letter A – and use the I-beam to draw out a small rectangle. This is a text field, a small part of your drawing document that thinks it's a word processing file.

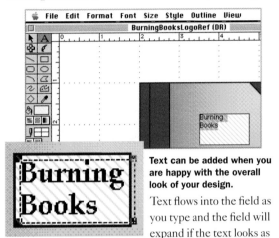

Text can be added when you are happy with the overall look of your design.

Text flows into the field as you type and the field will expand if the text looks as though it might overflow. You can select a text field in a drawing document, in the usual way, and it will grow handles that allow it to be stretched or moved. You can just click with the I-beam where you want to start typing and the field will expand in a similar way. To reformat text, drag the I-beam cursor over a section of it to select it. Once it is highlighted, choose a font by selecting from the pull down Size, Font and Style menus. (Notice that when you are working in a text field the word processing menu appears at the top of the screen. This menu bar always reflects the current environment.)

In the example the font selected was 22 pt Palatino Bold type in maroon. Notice that the text acts like any other object and can be picked up and dragged independently of the rest of the logo. But when you try to move only a small amount to float it in the middle of the nameplate, it automatically snaps back to its old position. This is because *ClarisWorks* has an automatic

grid that aligns objects to one or other of the points on the rulers at the top and side of the document window. If you don't see the rulers, select Show Rulers from the View menu.

To switch off the Autogrid, select Autogrid Off from the Options menu. Select the text box now and you can drag it anywhere you like.

To add a radius to the nameplate, double click on it and a dialog box will appear, prompting you for some dimensions. Type in 5 (the units are in typographical points) and hit OK. The effect of adding the radius may not be all that visible on screen, but it will be more pronounced when you print your document out.

Add a radius to any rectangle in the same way.

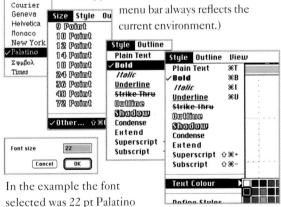

All these sharp edges can lead to a caustic look, so soften up.

As you discovered earlier, the multiple layers in an object can make life confusing, especially as you start to build up complicated designs. To simplify matters, now that the basic lines of the logo are in place, the next thing to do is to group the components together.

To do this, select the whole logo by dragging out a marquee, and choose Group from the pull down Arrange menu. (You can reverse this process at any time using the Ungroup command in the same menu.)

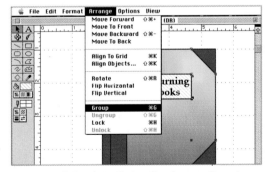

Now keep all the elements together for security and ease.

Now when you click on the logo only a single set of handles will appear and the number of layers is back down to one. Even more usefully, the logo now behaves as if it were a single object. For example, we can stretch the logo to make it look more like a journal.

82

An ominous footnote here is that this manoeuvre has not affected the type. This recalcitrant behaviour of type when resizing documents will give us a few more problems later on when we try to shrink the logo to a usable size, but thankfully there is a straightforward solution.

For now, we will finish off the basic design with a little fire and brimstone.

The best tool for creating an irregular object, such as a flame, is the Freehand tool. Select it from the tools palette in the usual way and experiment making a flame on the page. You may, at first, think it would be simpler to use two sticks, but you should persevere and soon you'll have the secret of man's red fire.

Once you've created the flame, watch out for something weird that happens to it when you release the mouse button. It immediately goes inexplicably limp. The culprit is *ClarisWorks*' automatic smoothing tool, another very helpful little gadget laid on by Claris for smoothing the often chaotic line art of the novice, but one that nevertheless would be appreciated a lot more if it didn't come configured as the default setting. To return the flames to their flickering glory, select Unsmooth from the pull-down Edit menu. When you're happy with the flame, click to select it and select the Gradient Fill tool from the Tools palette. Select a gradient that looks vaguely flame-like and voilà! – a pretty good flame. Repeat the process to create a smaller secondary flame using a slightly different fill.

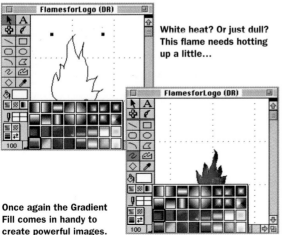

White heat? Or just dull? This flame needs hotting up a little...

Once again the Gradient Fill comes in handy to create powerful images.

Now here comes another clever bit.

Click on the smaller flame and drag it over the larger flame. Click on the pointer tool and drag out a marquee until the handles on both flames show they are both selected. Select White from the Pen Tool Colour palette to remove the object's outline. Notice your flame is now even more flame-like.

Select Group from the pull down Arrange menu.

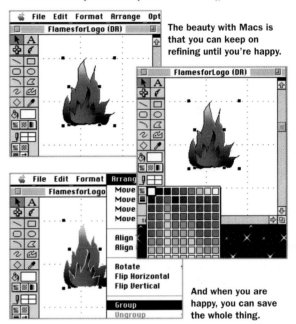

The beauty with Macs is that you can keep on refining until you're happy.

And when you are happy, you can save the whole thing.

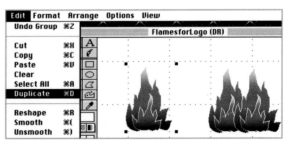

One object can easily be duplicated and then re-used.

Finally, select Duplicate from the pull down Edit menu. As the name suggests, this menu option duplicates whichever object is currently selected. A speedy alternative is to press Command-D. Press Command-D repeatedly and you will soon be up to your eyes in flames.

Experiment by combining them in different ways, moving objects backwards and forwards using the Move commands in the Arrange menu and generally trying to create a pleasing effect.

83

Once you are comfortable with these few basic manoeuvres, select a group and copy it to the Clipboard using the Copy command from the pull down Edit menu (the keyboard shortcut is Command-C).

Now return to the Burning Books logo and paste a copy of the flames in a clear space by pressing Command-V.

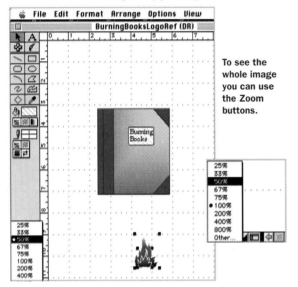

To see the whole image you can use the Zoom buttons.

You will see from the picture that the image has also been scaled down to give us more elbow room. Notice that the image still measures 3.5 in, by the vertical ruler. It is only the scale of the window that has changed.

To zoom in or out of a document, click on either of the two mountain icons (close and distant) at the bottom left-hand corner of the document window or click on the pop-up zoom menu to select a specific value.

To alter the physical size of an object, there are three different techniques. The simplest is just to grab its handles and pull. A more controlled way is to select Scale Selection from the pull down Options menu and to enter your own scale in the dialog box.

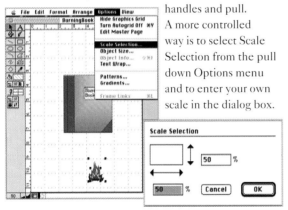

Re-scaling can be accurately achieved with this option.

An even more precise method is to select Object Size from the Options menu. The dialog box that appears here allows you to type in the exact dimensions of the object, and its position relative to the grid. The one you should use depends on how precise you need to be.

More entertainingly, you can also flip, rotate or align objects by choosing the appropriate menu option from the Arrange menu.

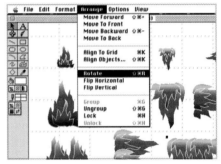

Now go crazy, after all that's what your imagination is for – and that's what the Mac's great at.

Using these few basic tools you can soon build up a vast repertoire of alternative designs very quickly. Save each one you choose to keep to the Documents folder under a different name.

Power *Tips* ....

AUTOSMOOTHING: if you want to disable the autosmoothing tool for the duration, select Preferences from the Edit menu, and uncheck the box marked 'Automatically Smooth Freehand'. Then hit OK.

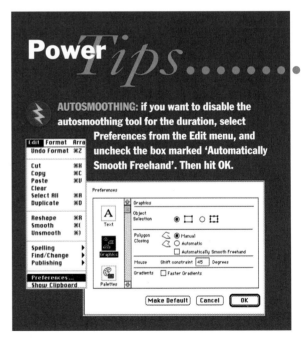

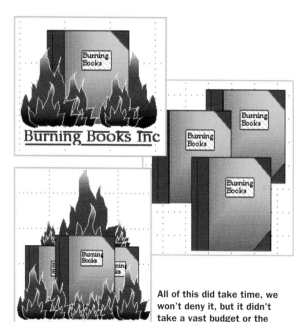

All of this did take time, we won't deny it, but it didn't take a vast budget or the advice of a design agency. Pretty impressive huh?

The company banner was added to each of the logos using the same techniques that were used earlier to create a text field for the nameplate, and again colour was added by highlighting the text and selecting Text Colour from the Style menu. But now we have a number of designs finalised there still remains the problem of the recalcitrant type. As we saw earlier, when an object is reduced in a drawing document, the embedded font does not alter with it. This has the unfortunate effect that when we shrink the logo the text makes a break for it.

Watch those keylines.

The solution is to save two copies of the document. The first is our working design in *ClarisWorks* format. The second, which we will save as a PICT file, will be the final logo. PICT is a graphical file format that is commonly used by Mac applications for transferring scalable images from one package to another.

Select Save As… from the pull-down File menu, and when the Save As… dialog box appears give your PICT logo a distinctive and obvious name. Calling it LogoPICT ought to distinguish it clearly from the ClarisWorks Drawing document. Ensure the Save As…

dialog box is set to PICT and then hit Save.

Save the working version as well, by pressing Command-S, and then click the close button at the top left-hand corner of the title bar. Now open the PICT version by double clicking its icon in the Documents folder.

Go back to the Options menu, choose Scale Selection, and scale the horizontal and vertical axes to 25 per cent. Voilà! – a small but perfectly formed logo.

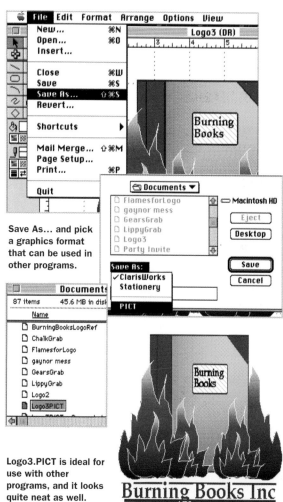

Save As… and pick a graphics format that can be used in other programs.

Logo3.PICT is ideal for use with other programs, and it looks quite neat as well.

✚ DON'T PANIC
PICT files print much better than they appear on screen.

Now you have your valuable logo in *ClarisWorks* Drawing and PICT formats it is a good idea to store a third copy to the Mac's Scrapbook. The Scrapbook is the most convenient place to store frequently used graphics because from here you can quickly copy and paste them into any other document.

Click on the reduced PICT logo and press Command-C to copy it to the Clipboard. The Clipboard is the usually hidden scratchpad area the Mac uses for storing images during cutting and pasting. Open the Scrapbook by selecting it from the pull down Apple menu.

Select Paste from the Edit menu or press Command-V and your logo is permanently saved to the Scrapbook.

The Mac's Scrapbook comes in handy once again. Saving your Pict here means you can use it in other programs.

It can be called up at any time by selecting Scrapbook from the Apple menu.

If you now want to paste it from here to a word processing document or template, as outlined in Chapter 6, just click on the area in the word processing document where you want the image to appear, and press Command-V. Your document will be enlivened at once.

Your newly created logo sits well in your WP documents too.

HOW TO Edit Colours

Patterns and Fills

You have seen in this chapter how powerful *ClarisWorks*' fill tools and effects can be, but you may find that the number and the choice of colours and fills is a bit limiting. Fortunately, extending and customizing the palette is very simple.

To change from a fixed 81 colour palette to a 256 colour editable palette, choose Preferences from the pull down Edit menu, and double click on Palettes in the left-hand column of the Preferences dialog box.

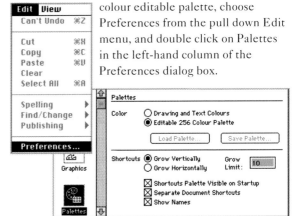

These preferences are yours to do with as you so desire.

The contents of the dialog box change to show you the current Palettes Preferences. Tick the box marked 'Editable 256 Colour Palette' and then hit OK.

Editing Palettes

Return to your Drawing document, and you will find that when you select the Pen Colour or Fill tools, a 256 colour palette now appears. By keeping the mouse button depressed, you will find you are able to tear off and move these palettes to a different part of the screen.

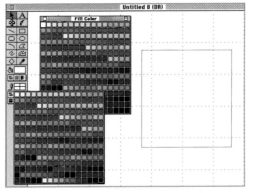

Each individual hue and shade can be edited to suit you.

This goes for the pattern and gradient palettes as well. Once you have torn off a palette, double click on any square and you will be able to edit its colour and, where appropriate, its gradient or pattern.

To edit a colour, click inside the colour wheel on any colour you want to sample. When you are happy, click OK. To edit a pattern, click in the sample area to toggle a pixel on and off.

Gradients are a little more involved, because they have a focal point and a number of colours. Nevertheless, you will find the controls very intuitive. Just click and drag until you get a result you are happy with and again hit OK.

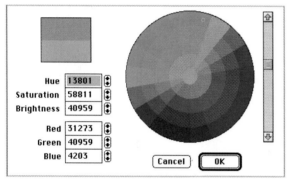

This wheel enables you to develop shades to your taste.

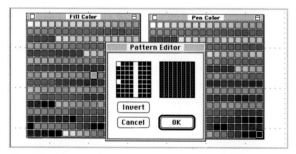

Even the patterns are not sacred, you can change these too.

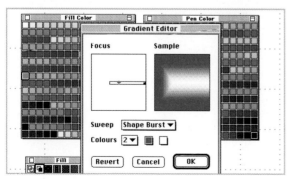

With practice you can make incredibly impressive gradients.

HOW TO Paint by Numbers

At first sight, the Painting environment looks much more attractive than the Drawing environment. Not only does it give you access to all the tools in the Drawing tool palette, it gives you a whole lot more besides, including brushes, spray cans, pencils, free rotation, tools for perspective, distortion and shear and colour manipulation tools such as Invert and Blend.

The drawback is that a paint document is much less flexible to work with, because rather than separate objects it is made up thousands of tiny picture elements (pixels) that only exist as single blobs. Each environment has its own distinct advantages and disadvantages as will soon become clear.

Individual components can't be treated as separate objects in the way they are in a Drawing document, so Drawing gives you a great deal of control and flexibility when it comes to editing documents. But Drawings can be imported to Painting documents and manipulated to fantastic effect.

In the following example we're going to create an aquarium, using Painting tools extensively. But first we are going to create the fish using the Drawing environment.

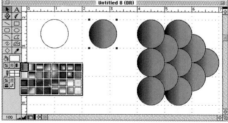

A Circle tool can be used to build complex patterns for further work.

 The picture above shows how the Circle tool, and a simple graduated fill can be used to create the appearance of a 3-dimensional fish scale. Use the Grouping, Duplication and Fill tools to diversify.

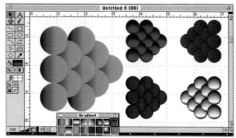

These patterns can be improved with gradients.

Then use the Arc and Circle tools to give the fish some character. Select the Arc and Circle tools from the tools palette, and use them to build the shape of fins and tails by alternately adding arcs and circles and then masking off unwanted details.

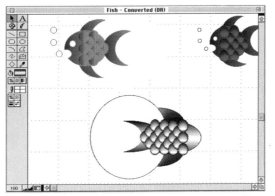

Using normally dry geometric tools can create strange images.

Once you are happy with the inhabitants of your aquarium group the components of each fish in turn, using the Group command from the Arrange menu. This stops them falling apart at the gills when you move them around the screen.

Now select the entire image, by choosing Select All from the Edit menu (or pressing Command–A). To reduce them to a more manageable size, select Scale Selection from the Options menu, choose 50 x 50 % and hit OK.

A graphical aquarium produced with a few basic ideas!

Your raw fish are now in place. Select Save As from the File menu and rename the file something obvious, like FinishedFish, in *ClarisWorks* format. Don't close the Drawing document just yet, though. First you need to copy it to the Clipboard from where you can copy it to the Painting document.

88

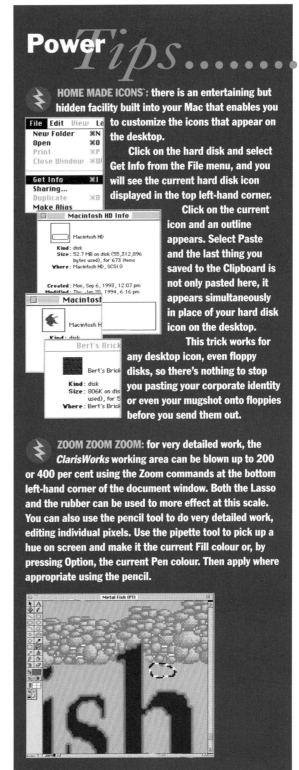

Power*Tips*........

HOME MADE ICONS: there is an entertaining but hidden facility built into your Mac that enables you to customize the icons that appear on the desktop.

Click on the hard disk and select Get Info from the File menu, and you will see the current hard disk icon displayed in the top left-hand corner. Click on the current icon and an outline appears. Select Paste and the last thing you saved to the Clipboard is not only pasted here, it appears simultaneously in place of your hard disk icon on the desktop.

This trick works for any desktop icon, even floppy disks, so there's nothing to stop you pasting your corporate identity or even your mugshot onto floppies before you send them out.

ZOOM ZOOM ZOOM: for very detailed work, the *ClarisWorks* working area can be blown up to 200 or 400 per cent using the Zoom commands at the bottom left-hand corner of the document window. Both the Lasso and the rubber can be used to more effect at this scale. You can also use the pencil tool to do very detailed work, editing individual pixels. Use the pipette tool to pick up a hue on screen and make it the current Fill colour or, by pressing Option, the current Pen colour. Then apply where appropriate using the pencil.

HOW TO **Alter Graphics**

To open a Painting document, select New from the pull down File menu, then click Painting in the New document dialog box. Then hit OK.

When the blank document appears, select Paste from the Edit menu or press Command-V. The saved FinishedFish appears inside a dotted border,

Pasting once again, it's a Mac staple.

indicating the area of the painting that is currently selected. As you will discover, selecting individual objects in a painting environment is a completely new proposition.

In the early stages, when there is still plenty of white space on the screen, there is still no problem. To select a fish, click on the dotted Rectangular Selection tool in the toolbar and use it to enclose a single fish. Pressing the Command key at the same time effectively shrinkwraps the dotted line round the object, allowing you at this stage to handle it in much the same way as you would an object in a Drawing file. Once the fish is selected it can again be duplicated by selecting Duplicate from the Edit menu, or resized by selecting Resize from the Transform menu.

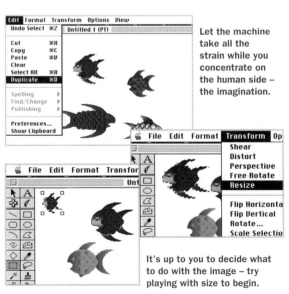

Let the machine take all the strain while you concentrate on the human side – the imagination.

It's up to you to decide what to do with the image – try playing with size to begin.

Using the same techniques, you can also rotate or distort an image, using a variety of image manipulation tools available in the Transform menu.

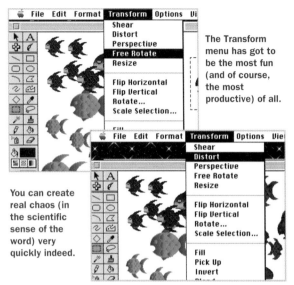

The Transform menu has got to be the most fun (and of course, the most productive) of all.

You can create real chaos (in the scientific sense of the word) very quickly indeed.

As things start to get crowded, you may find it is impossible to use the rectangular selection tool, without ensnaring sundry tails and fins of other fish. This is where the Lasso tool comes in.

Select the Lasso by clicking in the tool palette in the usual way. Use the tip to carefully draw around the image you want to select and as long as the background is still white you can use it to shrinkwrap individual fish and also to shrinkwrap images in groups.

Using the Lasso tool enables you to carry out precise selections.

Manipulate your design until you are happy with the basic layout, then save your work.

Select Save As from the File menu, give the file an appropriate name, make sure the dialog box header is set to Documents, and hit OK.

Now comes the tricky bit. We are going to add a paint fill to give some perspective to the fish tank. The problem is that once a paint fill has been applied all the individual images overlap and it is almost impossible to disentangle them. Unlike in Drawing documents, it is not possible to click on an object to select it. There is no such thing as an object in a paint document. For this reason it is important to save your work after each stage, so that if things do go horribly wrong you can revert to the last saved version.

We are now going to do some freehand painting to add a few pebbles to the bottom of the tank. This is quite an easy job, but before starting anything in the paint environment, always remember to set up Pen and Colour Fill attributes as there is no prospect of changing them afterwards short of rubbing out and starting again. When you use a tool, anything you draw takes on the current attributes. In the picture below, the Pen was set

Forget geometric tools – draw freehand.

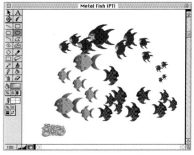

up for a 1pt Gold line and an edited gradient was selected for the Fill Tool. Notice the pebbles take on these colours immediately you draw. To save time, try drawing just a small area, then use the Lasso and the Duplicate command to cover the bottom of the whole tank.

One small element can be used to build the big picture.

HOW TO Add the Finish

Sooner or later you are going to start itching to pour on a background colour. Be warned, adding a background fill too early creates more problems than it solves. It is a bit like moving into a new house and laying the carpet before you've painted the shelves – it looks great, for about ten minutes.

Ideally the background fill should be one of the last things to go in. In this example, however, we're going to add it now, to highlight some of the problems that can occur.

To add a background fill, select the fill colour from the Fill Colour palette; then click on the Paint Fill tool (there are two bucket icons in the Painting tools palette – the lower one is where you specify the fill colour and the one higher up, to the right, is for applying it). Now move the bucket icon over to any area of white space and click.

You may find that some areas don't fill properly because they are enclosed by overlapping images. Touch each in turn with the hot spot of the bucket – the pouring paint part – and it will fill as advertised.

Handle the Fill tool with care. Ideally it should be used last.

Notice that when you use the Lasso now, the noose won't tighten over a particular area. That is because,

with the colour everywhere, it doesn't know what the intended area is. Also, when you move the lassoed area now, it leaves a hole. This is not necessarily a problem; the hole can be refilled using the same technique we used to fill the screen in the very first place.

Holes can be filled.

It just makes life a bit more complicated.

For our next trick we are going to add a few fronds of seaweed and assorted flotsam to the tank, using the Paint Brush and Spray Can tools. To select the brush tool, click on the icon in the usual way. Double clicking on either the Brush icon or the Spray Can icon opens a dialog box that enables you to customise the tool before you use it.

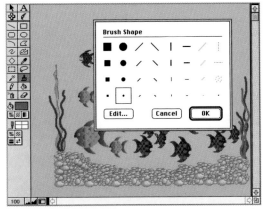

And you thought brushes went out when the Mac came in.

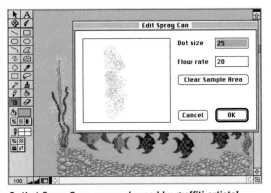

Or that Spray Cans were only used by graffiti artists!

The paint brush and the spray can work in a similar way, although the effect is different. Brush strokes have a coarse, dense texture, while spray paint covers a wider area and is more diffuse. Nevertheless, each uses the colour currently selected from the palette to make an indelible mark on the screen. As ever, when using these tools it is important to remember to select the colour attributes before selecting the tool.

To finish off the design, we are going to put a text box inside the tank to name the fish we have created. But first we need to clear some white space. If we were to create a text field against the filled background it would be almost impossible to select the text properly to apply special effects.

To recreate white space, click on the dotted rectangle tool and use it to pull out a marquee. Then hit delete.

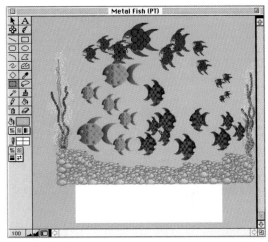

An easy way to create some space in which you place text.

Click on the Text tool – the letter A in the Tools palette – and use the I-beam to draw out a respectable-sized rectangle. A flashing cursor appears in the text box to indicate that the text box is selected. Now select a typeface from the Font menu as well as the type size, the type style and the type colour, before you start typing.

Even though it's a paint package you can still add some choice words.

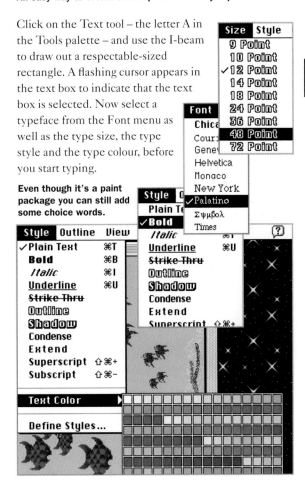

Type your heading. Use the rectangular selection tool, pressing Command at the same time, to shrinkwrap the heading. Choose Perspective from the Transform menu and use the handles to make the heading look as if it's coming out of the page.

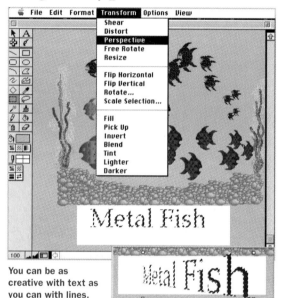

You can be as creative with text as you can with lines.

Click outside the heading to deselect the Perspective tool and click again to deselect the heading. Only deselect the heading once you are sure you are finished. As long as it's inside its white box and you still have it selected it continues to act like an object, a little bubble of order in a sea of chaos. Once you click outside the box it becomes just another bitmap and will probably prove difficult to lasso a second time.

Fill in the remaining white areas using the Paint Fill tool (the bucket again). Then select Blend from the Transform menu. This tool blends the edges of the two contrasting colours together and adds to the impression of depth again.

Finally, blend the text with the picture.

There are a number of other effects that we could have tried, but using all of them would have made the design too fussy. Here is a lightning tour of the effects that we haven't mentioned so far. They were achieved by selecting, respectively, Invert, Lighter and Darker from the Transform menu.

You can go back to your saved file if anything goes awry.

Finding that perfect finish is a case of trial and error.

These different lighting effects can be used to add drama.

You can design your way out of all recognition however.

But don't let this stop you from stretching your ideas fully. This last one was created by selecting Duplicate and Flip Horizontal and then scaling to 50%.

When you are finally happy with your design, hit Save (Command-S) and your masterpiece is saved to the hard disk.

Before you close, you probably also want to print out your design to see what it likes like on hard copy. Printing is very straightforward once your printer has been set up properly and selected from the chooser. If you haven't set up your printer yet, consult the manual that came with it together with Chapter 11 of this book. To find out how to initialize a printer, turn to the Chooser section in Chapter 4.

Once you're set up and ready to go, select Print from the pull down File menu. You will see the standard Print dialog box.

Hit Print and then go for a coffee and a donut because bitmap documents take much longer to print than text documents. When you come back, your fish should be ready.

The final masterpiece created with few good ideas and a Mac.

Power*Tips*

I CAN'T REMEMBER: memory problems are very common with paint applications because paint files tend to be so large. If your Mac repeatedly tells you there is not enough memory to perform a particular operation, this could well be because *ClarisWorks* does not have enough RAM allocated to it.

To allocate more memory, find the *ClarisWorks* application icon in your Applications folder, click on it once and select Get Info from the File menu.

In the Get Info dialog box, where it says preferred memory size, type in 2048. This should be enough for most reasonable-sized documents

If the problem persists, it could be that you simply don't have enough RAM to run *ClarisWorks* effectively. One way around this is to turn over part of your hard disk to operate as RAM. This operation, known as setting up Virtual Memory, is set out in detail in Chapter 3.

HOW MANY DOTS? In the *ClarisWorks* Paint environment, the resolution and colour depth of a document is preset to 72dpi (dots per inch) and 256 hues. If you have a 300dpi printer and a substantial amount of memory installed in your Mac, you can increase the resolution and the number of hues that can be displayed in a given document. Select Resolution and Depth from the Format menu and click the preferred values in the dialog box.

But be warned that a 300dpi image measuring 6¼ in x 6¼ in (that is 2000 x 2000 pixels) with only 256 colours requires a whopping 13Mb of memory. And if you have less it will probably never open.

Databases

A system *that works like a filing cabinet and filing clerk rolled into one*

9

Databases make people nervous, but they are no more than collections of related information. A phone book is an example of a database; a personal address book or contacts book, like a personal organiser, is another; product information electronically entered at a check-out is a third.

Database management packages on the Mac enable electronic collections of records (the database) to be manipulated so the information they hold can be sorted and accessed in useful ways.

Strictly speaking all the database applications on the Mac are actually database managers rather than databases; people build databases using the application to input their data.

Why use them?

Databases can be used for any job that requires information to be gathered, stored and then manipulated so it can be viewed and accessed in different forms. The beauty of electronic databases is that they are much more flexible than paper-based versions. Take a phone book, for instance. In printed form it's useful only if you know the exact name and often the address of the person you want to ring – you can't, for example, search by phone number. The advantage of an electronic database is that it allows you to search by the information you do know, and sort by that information too.

Despite that, the basic tenets of paper-based systems hold true. A useful way to consider how Mac databases work is to regard the system as a filing cabinet and filing clerk rolled into one.

The cabinet is your Mac loaded with a database program like *ClarisWorks* or *FileMaker Pro*. Within each folder in this cabinet are different sets of related information – different databases; for example, information about clients, information about objects, information about a business, or information about a specific activity.

Within the folder, different record cards will hold information about specific subjects, about an individual client, an individual object, or an individual project. This information can itself be broken down into different categories – say price, cost, date of acquisition, address, or phone number. Each of these smaller details – categories of information – are called fields. Records and Fields are the basic building blocks of databases, understand that and you're half-way there. The filing clerk, by the way, is the application itself, which will fetch you different records and organize them in different ways.

A simple address list can be part of a powerful database.

Here is an address database; we've used the database option in *ClarisWorks*. This contains 20 records, each with three fields – first name, second name, and address. Maureen Visigoth of Central Europe is the record selected at the moment – as indicated by the green highlight bar.

Records

All database documents are made up of records. Records consist of a series of fields. A Record means the complete set of information stored on a single 'record card'. You can sort, match and select records into groups for printing, mail merging, or researching.

Fields

Fields make up records. Fields can be defined to hold different kinds of data – in *ClarisWorks* you can define fields to hold text, numbers only, or more specific categories like time and date. You can also define fields in relation to others so they can perform calculations based on data entered in other fields. For example, it is possible to set up a field which will add up the numbers in a set of other fields and come up with a total. You can also use functions to define more sophisticated relationships between fields.

There are other criteria you can apply to fields. For example, you can specify that they will accept data from a pre-selected list of names, or that the numbers they accept are above or below set limits. If you set up your fields right, your database will work. Take care of the fields and the data will take care of itself.

Information typed into the database is poured into a structure dictated by how you have set up the fields within the records. (There are many databases where a professional has set up this structure – in which case you are pouring information into their pre-determined mould. Automated Teller Machines are a good example of this.)

An example of a field: someone's first name in the book.

On screen, 'fields' are the slots where information can be added.

How to define a record from the start-point of a database.

Choose the type of field you want, and give it a name – that will appear on your database. You are also given the choice of further defining your options. When you've finished, click Done.

Power*Tips*..........

AS SIMPLE AS A-TO-Z: however you view it, information in a database is retained in a constant relationship to other data. You may choose to view only the A–Ds of a particular database. That doesn't mean the E–Zs aren't there.

It's simply a question of how you want to see it. Think of layouts as a way of displaying information on show, as well as a way of presenting it visually as page layout. You're not changing how information is stored within your Macintosh, all you are actually doing it editing the relationship between it by showing it in a particular way.

FLAT-FILE OR RELATIONAL?: the difference between database applications is effectively how flexibly information can be manipulated and displayed once it has been entered; another centrally defining factor is how efficiently your data is stored once it has been entered.

There are two kinds of database: Flat-File or Relational. In a flat-file database all the information itself and the information about how it is organized is held on one file. For general information-management tasks, a flat-file database is simpler and more appropriate.

A relational database can handle more complex relations between different blocks of information because the records – that is, the information – are held on a number of different files that can talk to each other via a database manager.

ClarisWorks includes a flat-file database while *FileMaker Pro*, also by Claris, is flat-file but with some relational capabilities.

At the high end there are databases such as *4D* and *Omnis* which are relational. They tend to be used by professional developers to build databases to do specific jobs for groups of less skilled users.

Unless you are thinking of producing a seriously high-end database to cater for 1,000s of kilobytes of intense data, *ClarisWorks* or *FileMaker Pro* will easily be adequate for your needs at the moment.

Layout, Browse and Find

Records and fields are the genotype for the way files are stored in your database. Once you've set it up you can edit the way you enter, view, print and present data in different ways – in *ClarisWorks* via three commands: Layout, Browse and Find.

You can search the database you've set up in a layout, using a Browse or Find command to look through different layouts.

HOW TO Get Started

Using databases is a variation on a very simple theme, once you understand the metaphor. The details are tricky, however – small changes in formula, printing glitches, working out how to set variations can trip you up until you are familiar with an application.

So here we go. This workthu' explains how to build an address book. One good thing about databases is that they're imitable: use this for any simple database involving numbers but not calculations.

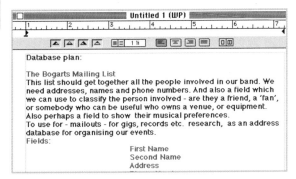

An element of forward planning is essential for success.

First plan it. It's easier to get the structure right first time around. Write a list of the fields you need and what you want them to do – and include everything you may need. You don't have to include all categories in every view of your data. In this example, a database contacts book for a band, it makes sense to define fields for first and second names. Consider also whether you want a separate field for the post or zip code.

You'll need to open *ClarisWorks* in database mode. The general principles we are about the describe in this section will also apply to most flat file databases including *FileMaker Pro*.

ClarisWorks takes you straight to a Define Fields box. To define your fields type each one in turn into the Name slot. Decide what file type to select – in this case, Text. Click Create and the field will appear in the Define Fields box. The Options button enables you to further define the type of field you want, but ignore it for the moment. Don't hit Done when you've entered a field. Simply type the next field in and define it – use the command key shortcuts at the side of the field type boxes to speed up the operation as you get used to them.

For the most part you will enter field data as plain text.

If you make a mistake and you want to delete a field hit Delete. Note that this will destroy the field and any contents already entered – important to remember if you edit this box later.

As you can see, there are other entry formats available to you.

Back gracefully out of this dialog box to retain the Likes, Dislikes field. The address fields should be defined as Text.

You should also use Text (which means text and numbers) to define a phone number – this is because if you don't it will chop off any leading zeroes. When all the options are added, click Done.

You have now created a database with six fields. It looks rather disappointing because there aren't any records in it yet and it hasn't been formatted. *ClarisWorks* automatically opens the first record in the database. On the left is a book icon indicating which record is open – in this case 1. This also states how many records there are, and whether they are sorted.

Records: 1
Unsorted

The database is in Browse mode. You can verify this by looking under the Layout menu – where Browse

rather than Layout will be selected in the first quartile of options. Clear? That's because Claris should fix the dialog. To make everything even more obvious, your database is in Layout 1 – note the tick at the bottom of the box. The difference between Browse and Layout modes is that Layout allows you to organize how you enter, view and present information. Browse allows you to view and search your database. Layout is for when you are setting up or editing your database. Browse is really for using it. You can add new records in either mode.

Untitled 5 (DB)

First Name	Billy
Second	McInnes
Address	London Fields
Phone	ex directory
Who Are	Band Member
Likes,	Rockabilly

Records: 1

Layout mode won't affect the data, only the way it looks.

For the meantime fill in the first record. Tabbing from field to field is quicker than selecting. If you select outside the field areas, you'll select the whole record. Click inside a field to deselect.

Edit Format Layout
Can't Undo	⌘Z
Cut	⌘X
Copy	⌘C
Paste	⌘V
Clear	
Select All	⌘A
New Record	**⌘R**
Duplicate Record	⌘D
Copy Summaries	

To add more records go to the Edit menu and choose New Record or use Command-R. Add as many records as you have records to add in this way – naturally you can add records at any point... (Some of the titles of the fields – for example, Likes and Dislikes – are truncated. To fix this this turn to the

First Name	Jay
Second	Dead
Address	Notting Hill Gate
Phone	Never answers the phone
Who Are	Music Critic
Likes,	Free Lunches, Dislikes all music.

section on Layouts later in the chapter.)

The index at the side of the screen keeps a tab of the number of records in the database. Moving the bookmark will take you through different pages.

Records: 5
Unsorted

Your database works and has records in it. If you want to customize your layout switch from Browse to Layout (under the layout menu). You'll see how your database is laid out. The graphic tools to change it are down the left-hand side, and in the menu bars.

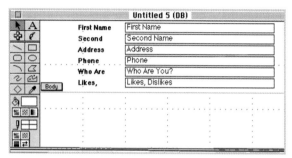

On the left are the tools you can use to smarten up the look.

Choose New Layout from the Layout menu. And name your layout in the dialog box this brings up. There are various options for different layouts. We used Columnar.

New Layout

Name Band MailOut List

Type
○ Standard ● Columnar report
○ Duplicate ○ Labels
○ Blank Custom ▾

[Cancel] [OK]

You can use templates for the creation of future databases. Get into the habit, because they do make life a great deal easier.

You can show information on a layout in any order. It depends which of the defined fields you choose to Move first. Do this by selecting and clicking Move. If you don't want all the fields to appear don't Move them. They stay with the database but not this view of it. Here we chose only the two name fields and the address.

Set Field Order

Field List		Field Order
First Name	[Clear]	First Name
Second Name		Second Name
Address	« Move «	Address
Phone		
Who Are You?	[OK]	
Likes, Dislikes	[Cancel]	

You can quickly re-arrange the way in which the data appears.

Databases

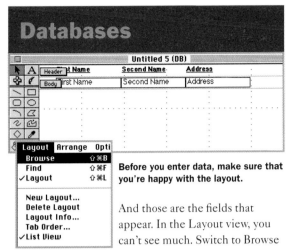

Before you enter data, make sure that you're happy with the layout.

And those are the fields that appear. In the Layout view, you can't see much. Switch to Browse and you'll see your Band mail out list – your database has been customized so you see what you need.

Then enter small amounts as tasters for the finished database.

But there's lots that can still be done by selecting text and colouring it – under the Style menu. Use the fill palette for colouring boxes. Style might be the wrong word, but at least each category stands out. Notice each record is highlighted as you select it (here in green).

This gives you the chance to make any final tweaks.

Finally, save your database – this saves both the layouts and the database records. Don't quit the program if you've added records but don't like the look of your layout or you will lose all the work defining fields and any records you have added.

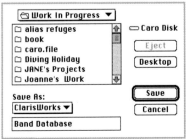

Searching a database

One way to navigate a database is to use the tools provided to flick through record by record. In *ClarisWorks* the book tool at the left of the screen means the database can be browsed page by page – each page of the book represents a single record and can be clicked on to select it. Or use the bookmark inserted in the side to give a rough indicator of how far through the database you want to look.

This presupposes that the database has been sorted in an order that makes this type of search rational – if no sort has been done the database will appear in order of entry. (In the screen shot below, note that the database hasn't been sorted at all yet.)

Now to test the water... retrieving data is the point of it all.

Find and Send

An easy way of searching for records is to use the Find command located under the Layout menu. This will search the database or section of it in a selected layout. (In this case, for example, we're looking at a layout called Band Mailout List. This shows only three fields, first name, second name and address; the root database holds more fields – phone number, who are and Likes – we're simply not showing them.)

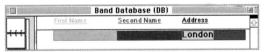

Even the simplest looking database can come in handy.

Clicking on Find brings up a Find Request; this looks like a blank record, and is in the same format as your own database. Use this to insert your search criteria – what you want the database to look for (hit return to activate the search). Here, London was the only criterion used at first, but the search could have been narrowed down adding different criteria in different fields – adding a surname in this case. Once the search has been completed the sidebar gives information on the number of records and then the number of finds – two in this case.

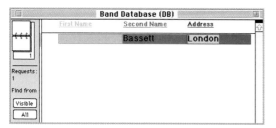

Searching out the right data turns into a skill after a while.

Because you can simplify or complicate your techniques.
You can take your search a stage further by looking only at visible records, that is, records you have already selected. So, in this example search first to find all the database entries who are music critics, Command-Shift-F, or Find under the Layout Menu, then set this search criteria in the Who Are You? field. Hit return or select All in the side panel. Five records were found. If these need to be sorted still further, simply select Find again,

The more complex the search pattern, the more connections.

Or you can simplify your search techniques for quick retrieval.
and add the new criteria – in this case we looked for London in the address field. Then click on Visible to sort only the 'visible' records – these are the records previously selected (you can't actually see them when you're setting search criteria).
If you want to start a new search – select Show All Records from the Organise menu; this brings back the full record set.

This list could be printed out – using Print under the File menu – mail merged, or you could work with it on screen. (For mail merge see the chapter on working with words.)

Search and Search Again

Another way to search is to stack up search requests – this would allow you to compile a list adding one Find request to another to produce an inclusive mail shot for a specific event relevant to two categories. To do this make one search request, but before hitting return or the Visible or All buttons, call up a new search request. To do this select New Request under the Edit menu. (If it's not there, check you have Find selected in the Layout menu.) You can make different search requests in the same field. The number of records selected as suitable is shown.

Sort It!

When you sort records, you are changing the order of the entire database – this means that record numbers will change if you change a sort. You can change the priorities by which records are selected, and within that process choose whether records are sorted in ascending (A–Z) or descending (Z–A) order.

To do it select Sort Records by dragging and clicking under the Organise menu. This brings up the Sort dialog box with a list of fields on the left and the Sort Order on the right. To determine a new sort order highlight the category you want to sort by and click Move – it hops across to the other side. Choose ascend or descend. To take a sort choice out, select it and hit Move again; it will disappear from the Sort Order box.

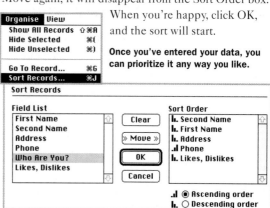

When you're happy, click OK, and the sort will start.

Once you've entered your data, you can prioritize it any way you like.

Power*Tips*

⚡ **FIELD HOPPING:** you can automate moving from field to field across records using a keyboard shortcut. Hit Command-R and you'll hop to the same field (for example, the Name field) in the next record. Pressing Command-Shift-Return enables you to quickly hop backwards from the particular field in one record to the same field in the previous record.

You need to be in Find mode rather than Browse or Layout to do this. The point of a database is, of course, so you can sort and view records in different combinations and in different orders.

Simple databases enable navigation through records you have already set up, in order to find required data quickly and easily. They also enable searches to be made to specific criteria and enable groups of records to be flagged and worked on as a discrete group.

⚡ **MULTIPLE REQUESTS:** broaden the selection criteria; choosing more than one field in a single search narrows it down.

⚡ **'GO TO' HINT:** save time with the Go To command. This is under the same menu as Sort – if you know a record's number, use it to go straight there (but remember, numbers will change if you change the sort criteria).

> **Go to record** ⎸5⎸
>
> [Cancel]   [**OK**]

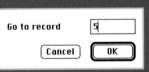

Hide After Seek

You can hide everything but the records you chose via the Hide tool in the Organise menu (make sure you're in Browse or you won't see this). You now know how to build a text database and interrogate it – that is, find and extract the information you need. The world is your digital filing cabinet.

HOW TO Database by numbers

The first database in this section used only Text and Date fields. Once they're on the page, you handle numbers pretty much like text. Number-based fields could be used if your database involves money. Number and text-based fields can also be more closely defined. You may want an intelligent date stamp, to keep track of joiners, or a way of limiting what can be inserted in a particular field – Yes or No, London or Liverpool, Tuesday or Wednesday – especially if a number of different people will actually do the inputting. This database was built using *ClarisWorks 2*. You can use most of the principles in other databases – for example, *FileMaker Pro*.

Here, we explain how to build a database using number, text and calculation fields to catalogue a collection of objects. We'll also look at how to define fields – including text fields – more precisely. Finally, we'll explain how to change the appearance of the database to suit the job in hand – and explain how you can use completely different Layouts with different information using the same basic database. First, open the database. Use the database module from *ClarisWorks*. Define the fields. In this case Artefact (define this as Text), Date Made (Date), date found (Date). Use the keyboard shortcuts as you get used to entering different types of data. They're next to the Field types.

A good database uses formats other than mere text.

Hit the Options button for Date Made and Date Found and it's possible to define the fields further. One Option here is to ensure that a field is completed. Here, Verify field data is checked for Not Empty. Your Mac will object if you try and leave this field vacant when entering records.

Entry Options for Date Field "Date Made"

Auto Entry
- ● No auto entry
- ○ Data
- ○ Variable — Creation Date ▼
- ○ Serial number
  - next value
  - increment

Verification — Verify field value is:
- ☒ Not empty
- ☐ Unique
- ☐ Range
  - from
  - to

Input List
- ☐ Pre-defined list — Edit List...
  - ☐ Only values from list

Cancel | OK

You can ensure that you don't forget to enter data.

Entry Options for Date Field "Date Found"

Auto Entry
- ○ No auto entry
- ● Data — 1/1/3001
- ○ Variable — Creation Date ▼
- ○ Serial number
  - next value
  - increment

Verification — Verify field value is:
- ☐ Not empty
- ☐ Unique
- ☐ Range
  - from
  - to

Input List
- ☐ Pre-defined list — Edit List...
  - ☐ Only values from list

Cancel | OK

You can also date-stamp every record if you so wish.

In Date Found we checked 1 January 3001 – this ensures the right date will appear in every record. Other fields are Finder – the people who found our twentieth-century time capsule; Value, which is a Number field; and Insurance, which will be a Calculation. Selecting Calculation will automatically open up a special options box. It looks daunting but it isn't. Insurance in this example is 10 per cent of the Value of the artefact. So this is what needs to be expressed in the Formula box.

Enter Formula for Field "Insurance"

Fields	Operators	Function
Artefact	+	ABS(number)
Date Made	-	ACOS(number)
Date Found	*	AND(logical1 ;logical2;...)
Finder	/	ASIN(number)
Value	=	ATAN(number)
Insurance	>	ATAN2(x_number ;y_number)
	<	AVERAGE(number1 ;number2 ;...)

Formula
'Value'/10

Format result as: Text / ✓Number / Date / Time

Cancel | OK

Calculation fields make for a very powerful set-up.

Above the input line are three resources to use. The Fields themselves; Operators – plus, minus, divide etc.; and Functions – the SUM of, for example. Effectively the idea is to take what you need. The Value field was chosen by double clicking in the box, a / was selected by clicking on it in the Operators box and the figure 10 for ten per cent was typed in. This tells *ClarisWorks* I want to put a number equal to ten per cent of the number in your value box in your insurance field in each specific record.

You could type the field name (in this case 'Value') in; if you do, remember to put it in single quotes. It's better to select and double click for accuracy's sake. The result is a calculation that expresses the fact that insurance is ten per cent of the value of the object.

When you're satisfied, hit OK – if you have a bad formula, *ClarisWorks* will tell you so and you can try again.

Functions (which we do not need in this case) are bits of code that will perform functions – SUM, one of the most useful, means the sum total of whatever is defined (you'll see the same things in spreadsheets).

Values for "Text" field "Paid?"

Yes

No

Create | Modify
Cancel | Delete | Done

Limit the text entry to valid options.

It's possible to give text fields limited options for entry – here, limits are being set on the Paid Field through the same Options dialog box. The only acceptable entries in this Field will be Yes or No.

When you've entered all the fields click Done. The database will open in Layout mode with a basic set-up. A hint here

Layout	Arrange	Opti
Browse	⇧⌘B	
Find	⇧⌘F	
✓Layout	⇧⌘L	

is to look for drawing tools rather than the database Book tool to the left of the screen if you get confused.

Untitled 3 (DB)

Artefact	Artefact
Date Made	Date Made
Date Found	Date Found
Finder	Finder
Value	Value
Insurance	Insurance
Paid?	Paid?

100 | Page 1

If you're not happy with the layout, you can modify it again.

Date Format

○ 26/7/92
◉ Jul 26, 1992
○ July 26, 1992
○ Sun, Jul 26, 1992
○ Sunday, July 26, 1992

[Cancel] [**OK**]

It makes sense at this point to make sure all the fields are properly set up. Double clicking on the text field will bring up other modify options. The date can be expressed in a number of forms; hit whichever makes most sense for the job in hand. Likewise all Number fields can be expressed as currency, percentages, general or other options. It's also possible to set levels of precision – number of places to divide to, for example.

Number Format

○ General   ☐ Commas
◉ Currency ☐ Negatives in ()
○ Percent
○ Scientific   Precision [2]
○ Fixed

[Cancel] [**OK**]

When you're happy with the definitions, move across to Browse mode and try out your new database by adding some records; for example, check the Calculation is right – it is in this example, as the insured amount has flashed up as 10 per cent of the value.

Untitled 3 (DB)

Artefact	Flared trousers
Date Made	Jul 30, 1966
Date Found	Thursday,
Finder	Ann Droid
Value	$ 2000.00
Insurance	$ 200.00
Paid?	No

Records: 1
Unsorted

Check any calculations before entering your main data.

You'll see that the database is presented in a very minimalist way. It's the basic List View, but all your fields are included.

Add some records using Command-R, or New Record under Edit when you're in the Browse mode.

Untitled 3 (DB)

Artefact	Flared trousers
Date Made	Jul 30, 1966
Date Found	Thursday,
Finder	Ann Droid
Value	$ 2000.00
Insurance	$ 200.00
Paid?	No
Description	Impractical youth ware. Revived 1990s. Yellow
Artefact	Shell Suit
Date Made	1989?
Date Found	Thursday,

Records: 11
Unsorted

100

From humble beginnings, you've now got a versatile database.

Now it can be tailored to suit different tasks. It can also be jazzed up so it's easier to view and access data. Open a New Layout by clicking on New Layout under the Layout menu. In this example the database must to do two things: provide a list of articles and a financial check, to ensure items are valued and insurance paid.

Power *Tips* ....

SELECTING IS A DRAG: a good way to select files is to drag-select them; keep the mouse depressed and pull across them – they will be highlighted. If you shift-click you can extend this choice. Command-click lets you deselect records within your selection. Here, highlighted files are still in the frame; the others have been deselected.

This is useful if you want to work through a database checking names rather than making a blind choice.

| 🍎 File | Edit | Format | Layout | Organise | View |

Band Database (DB)

First Name	Second Name	Address
Jay	Walker	Tokyo, Japan
Gui	Tan	Paris, Texas
Guy	Sneesby	Camden, London
Gonzo	Punk	Waterloo, London
Indy	Pendent	Camden Town,
Jake	Onthemake	North Beach, San
Billy	McInnes	London Fields
Joanne	Hurley	Toronto, Canada
Karen	Harvey	Highgate, London
Pen	Guin	Falkland Islands
Jay	Dead	Notting Hill London

Records: 17
Selected: 7
Sorted

FORMULA BASICS: keep fields in quotes. Remember brackets are calculated first – the answer to 2x(4 +4) = 16 – (2x8) – not 12 – (2x4+4).

HINT: test out formulae by checking they work on the first record they input. If you have to change them, it's better to do it early. *ClarisWorks* will tell you if your formula is bad, but not if it's wrong – for example, if you've divided the wrong way round.

HINT: try to select different parts and paste onto your calculation rather than writing them in; there's less room for error.

HINT: use the shortcut box under the Edit menu. It's a quick way to arrange records and to do certain edits – for example, cutting.

Shortcuts

The Layout therefore only includes four of the possible fields. Set field order by selecting and clicking Move in the order you want the fields to appear. To change them around you can Move backwards and forwards.

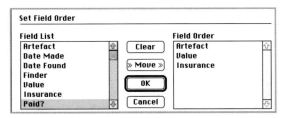

Format the data entry order to make it easier for you to work.

Our new layout appears. It needs a little customizing. Choosing text colour by dragging down the text box allows the text on the field labels to be customized – assuming that it has been selected (click with the pointer tool) first.

Now really start adding frills to make data access easier.

You can use the square tool from the toolbar to drag a background colour behind the fields too; select it and Send it to the Back or select the text and move it to the Front – find these options under the Arrange menu. Otherwise your square will sit on top of the text and obscure it. You can also put boxes around the fields, edit them using the line tools, and even add arrows. The colour palettes tear off from the menu for ease of use.

Boxing out fields makes data easier to see at a glance.

It's difficult to imagine how your layout is going to look from within Layout. New View under the View Menu enables you to look at the same Layout (remember a Layout is a way of interrogating the database, not simply the layout of it) in two modes. So here your financial database can be seen in Layout and in Browse mode – and you can see the effect of the rather violent purple and the arrows. You can also see clearly that not much of your twentieth-century memorabilia has been insured.

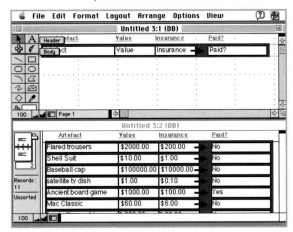

Remember, basically your database is an information provider.

HOW TO Summarize Info

This workthru' explains how to set up a database to run your personal finances. This involves using a final field definition – Summary – and also dividing your database into different parts by adding a header, and a grand summary, to the body containing the records themselves. Parts, used in *FileMaker Pro* as well as *ClarisWorks*, are a useful way of summarising and giving specific views of data – you drag information into different parts depending where you want to see them when you use the database on screen or printed out.

ClarisWorks includes a basic database that suits most everyday needs. Here we explain how to build a database to help keep track of your finances. Our model includes a simple in-out log, a running total and a details and reference section. The beauty of this database is that it is infinitely customizable and very simple once you've grasped the basics. This workthu' involves processes used right through this chapter. If you're confused you might want to refer back to the first few pages.

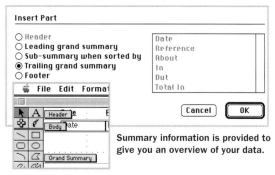

Set up a new database, this time using more than simple text entries.

Open *ClarisWorks* in database mode. Define your fields. These are the different entries you want included. We chose Date, Reference, About, In for money in and Out for money out. We also included Total In for money in, Total Out for money out and a Balance. Each field needs to be categorised as a Type according to the information it is to hold. Date is 'date', as the name implies, Info and About are text fields. In and Out are Number. All you do is click the applicable box. The only slight complications are Total In, Out and Balance. These are summary fields and need to be defined further.

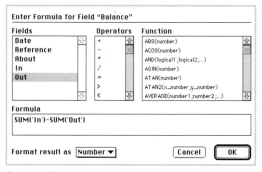

Don't be frightened of formulæ, they're there to help you.

It's easy. Type in Total In, check Summary in the Type box and you'll get a Formula dialog box. Total In is the Sum of all the entries you make under In. That is, all the money coming into your account. To express this so your database can understand it type SUM – the only piece of coding you're going to need to finish this task – then open a bracket, click on 'In' in the fields section or type it yourself, close the bracket and you're away. You should have typed SUM('In'). Ignore the function box to the right. Carry out the same procedure for Total Out. To enter the Formula for Balance just take Out away from In.

Back at the Define Fields box click Done. Your fields will appear on screen in a simple list view and you'll be in Browse mode. Select a Landscape option on Page Setup under the File menu. Then select New Layout under the Layout menu.

Chose Columns under the Set Up options and give your layout a name. You'll be prompted to set the field order.

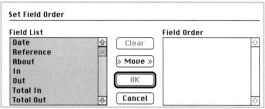

The Field order is important for your ease of use.

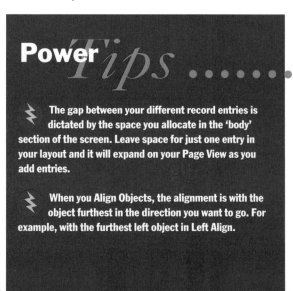

Summary information is provided to give you an overview of your data.

Finally, add a Trailing Grand Summary by choosing it on the Insert Part command under Layout. This is space to give you an overview of your account and the place to put Summary information.

Notice the Balance and Total In and Total Out fields don't appear. You need to insert them. Use Insert Field under the Layout menu to do this.

Power Tips

⚡ **The gap between your different record entries is dictated by the space you allocate in the 'body' section of the screen. Leave space for just one entry in your layout and it will expand on your Page View as you add entries.**

⚡ **When you Align Objects, the alignment is with the object furthest in the direction you want to go. For example, with the furthest left object in Left Align.**

Number Format

○ General   ☐ Commas
● Currency   ☐ Negatives in ()
○ Percent
○ Scientific   Precision [2]
○ Fixed

[Cancel]   [OK]

Keep your numbers to a minimum.

Select each of the number-based fields by clicking the body box, and use the Field Format command to state how the number should be expressed – either as currency or as a percentage, for example. For this workthu' check Currency.

Arrange your different fields by clicking and dragging the boxes. Titles to the fields should go in the Header, details in the Body, and Total In, Out and Balance in the Summary section of the sheet. Style and Align Object commands can be applied to anything you've selected to help tidy up the layout. (To select more than one object at once hold down the shift key and drag.)

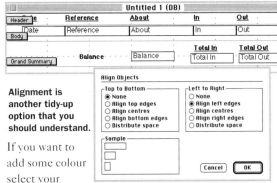

Alignment is another tidy-up option that you should understand.

If you want to add some colour select your boxes, then apply colours using the fill palette in the tool bar on the left of the Layout screen. Click the colour you want and it's applied to selected areas. To insert background colour (as along the top of the Header in the next shot) try experimenting with the square tool. You'll need to send it to the back so it doesn't cover your work – use the Arrange menu to do this.

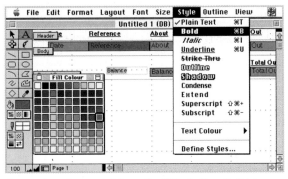

Can you have too much information? We don't really think so.

Reminders of regular financial commitments can be added in a text box in the summary area. You can add bold text or change font size or colour too. If you need to enlarge the summary box or any other area, drag the dividing line – the cursor turns into a cross bar.

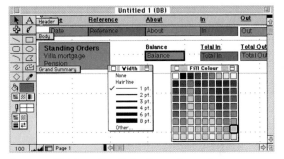

You can add information that will remain constant...

...by using box-outs on the database's 'work surface'.

When you're happy with the appearance choose Browse under Layout and then Page View under View. You've built yourself a simple system to keep track of your finances. Now Save As... a template.

Going back to your live file, to create records use Command-R, or New Record under the the Edit menu (in Browse mode). You'll need a new record for each transaction. Enter records in any order; you can sort them using Command-J, or Sort under the Organise menu. For a full view of your finances remember to use Page View in the View menu. To customize your layout switch to the Layout view. The net result should be that, unlike, the improvident Julius, you stay out of debt.

A simple database could help you to stay out of debt.

Spreadsheets

Analyzing *statistics, writing lists,* *creating* Home accounts

10

Spreadsheets have a reputation for complexity. This chapter is designed to dispel some of the misconceptions surrounding the spreadsheet which, in its simplest form, is no more than a flat-form table. Spreadsheets allow you to build tables very quickly, to set up powerful relationships between entries, or cells, and to generate graphs and charts automatically.

You can use spreadsheets for analysing football statistics, writing shopping lists, running the home accounts and even for double entry bookkeeping. What you do with your spreadsheet is between you and your conscience. Before you can do anything, however, you need to learn the tools of the trade.

The spreadsheet application used in this chapter is the spreadsheet environment in *ClarisWorks*, but you will find the tools are similar in most spreadsheet packages.

Class 3B Annual Report (SS)

H14

Class 3B	A	B	C	D	E	F	G	H
		Science						
	17/12/93	15/3/94	12/6/94	1/9/94	2/9/94	Total Score	Grade
	Assignment 1	Assignment 2	Assignment 3	Assignment 4	Written Test		
Arthur Anderson	83	71	90	85	45	86	
Bart Bacharach	61	59	60	65	28	59	
Ché Chesney	72	67	75	70	35	70	
Darren Dreen	75	74	80	76	16	54	
Eduardo Estrada	79	62	75	72	35	71	
Fulton Foster	94	82	89	95	49	94	
Gabriel Garcia	65	55	69	63	30	62	
Herbert Hestoff	21	30	5	7	16	24	
Inès Iquano	73	60	67	61	33	66	
Average Score per Assignment	69	62	68	66	32		

To launch *ClarisWorks*, double click on the *ClarisWorks* icon in your Applications folder.

The New Document dialog box appears automatically when you launch *ClarisWorks* and prompts you to select a document type. Click Spreadsheet and then hit OK.

If you are already working in *ClarisWorks*, select New from the pull down File menu to call up the dialog box.

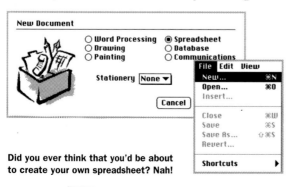

New Document

- ○ Word Processing   ● Spreadsheet
- ○ Drawing   ○ Database
- ○ Painting   ○ Communications

Stationery [None ▼]

[Cancel]

File **Edit** **View**

New...	⌘N
Open...	⌘O
Insert...	
Close	⌘W
Save	⌘S
Save As...	⇧⌘S
Revert...	
Shortcuts	▶

Did you ever think that you'd be about to create your own spreadsheet? Nah!

Again, click Spreadsheet and hit OK. The next thing you see will be an untitled Spreadsheet document. If the document window is too large, resize it by pressing the icon at the bottom right-hand corner of the window and dragging.

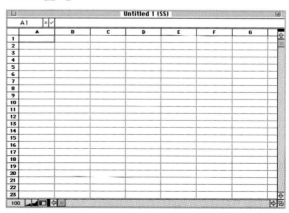

The naked sheet, sitting there just waiting for your figures.

The highlighted box is called a Cell – the home of your data.

ClarisWorks' Spreadsheet environment consists of a blank sheet of paper and tools for entering text and numbers, and mathematical and logical operators that allow you to build up complex relationships between cells.

We are going to create a spreadsheet that forms the basis of a Class Report, that could be used by a teacher or lecturer for logging students' term results and written tests, and automatically calculating their final marks.

Whatever the application, the first thing to do is to set up row and column headings.

Click the Spreadsheet cursor (shaped like a plus sign) on cell B2. That is the cell at the intersection of column B and Row 2. Type the words Assignment1. Notice the words appear in the Entry bar at the top of the spreadsheet and not in the cell itself.

Entering information into a cell is simply a case of typing.

To confirm the entry, click in the tick box next to the Entry bar or click in another cell. Click in cell C2 and type Assignment 2, or take a shortcut and click on cell B2, select Copy from the pull down Edit menu, click again on C2 and select Paste from the Edit menu. Click on D2 and E2, in turn, and repeat the procedure. This pastes Assignment 1 into all four cells, so obviously we need to change the number in each case. To edit the contents of a cell, click on it, use the I-beam cursor in the Entry window to highlight the elements you want to delete or edit and just type over the top.

You can even use good old copy and paste once again.

Fill-Down is a kind of turbo-charged Paste using a column.

To copy an entry from one cell to several adjacent cells, you can either copy and paste information individually, as above, or click on the cell you want to copy and select Fill Right or Fill Down from the Calculate menu.

If you make a mistake or you need a change, you can always add a new cell.

At this stage you realize that you need an extra layer of cells above Row 2 for the assignment dates. To insert a row of cells, click and then drag the cursor to highlight the row or column you want to move. Select Insert Cells from the Calculate menu, click on Shift cells down and hit OK. Notice the cell range B2–E2 has shifted down to B3–E3. Type in the Assignment deadlines using the same techniques as above.

You can even enter an entire new row of cells if needs be.

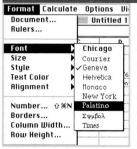

Entering text is constant with other Mac programs.

ClarisWorks' spreadsheet environment allows you to alter the Type, Size, Style and Colour of a font just as you would in any other *ClarisWorks* environment. To alter the typeface used in a cell, select the cell and then click on the pull down Format menu until Font is highlighted. When the Font sub-menu appears select Palatino.

Reformat Size, Style and Colour the text in exactly the same way.

If you choose a Size that is too big for the current cell, a series of hash signs may be returned. It is possible to resize the cell but, for now, just choose a smaller size.

Hash-marks mean that the text is too big for the cell.

Text alignment within cells is done via a menu.

You can also realign the data in a cell so that it is justified to the left of the cell, to the right or centred. Clicking on Wrap as well in this menu will force an entry that is too long to wrap around automatically to the line below, even if it belongs to another cell.

If you want the same attribute to apply to a series of cells, you can select an entire row or column or series of rows and columns and reformat them en masse. To select a row click on a start cell and drag the cursor until the cells you want to reformat are selected. Then repeat the reformatting steps outlined above.

It is quite possible to select more than one cell at a time.

108

The next stage is to enter the student's name in the column to the far left. Type in the first name and the chances are it will bust out of the cell.

Watch out for text that breaks the cell boundaries.

To make it wrap round, again choose Alignment from the Format menu and select Wrap from the sub-menu. The name will wrap round but you won't be able to see all of it unless you

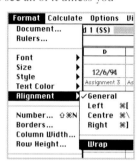

Select Wrap to ensure that text stays within the cell...

resize the cell. To increase the vertical dimensions of a cell, move the cursor to the left-hand margin and place it on the line that corresponds to the cell you want to extend (Row 4). The cursor changes to a paring tool which allows you to prise out some breathing space for the cell. Drag the line down to the next line on the grid and you should be able to see all of the name. Notice that every cell in the Row has changed at the same time.

...and you will find that your Mac tidies up for you.

You can stretch cells horizontally in exactly the same way.

You probably don't want to repeat this procedure for every single student on the register. To resize the entire first column, select it by clicking on the first cell and dragging, and then select Row Height from the Format menu. Type in a new Row Height of 26pt (there are 72 pts to an inch) and hit OK.

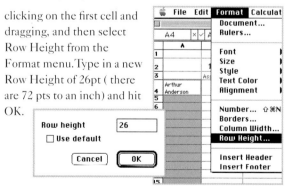

You can always re-define the height and width of a cell once you've defined it in the initial layout.

While you're at it, select Wrap from the Alignment sub menu so that every entry in the register wraps automatically and doesn't bust the cell.

Any spreadsheet worth the name will enable you to modify rows and columns in the same way as you would modify individual cells.

Key in the names of the entire class, just to prove it works, and then embolden the names.

As you can, the names of all the class members have been added and they all wrap within the text-holding cells. This makes for easier text entry in the future.

You can also take the hard work out of text-styling by highlighting entire columns of rows and then changing the lot in one go.

Add a new cell called Total Score and select Borders from the Format menu. When the Borders dialog box appears, click Outline and hit OK.

Adding borders to cells will make for a neat print-out.

The ability to makes radical changes to your basic spreadsheet is a philosophy and working practice that extends throughout all decent spreadsheet programs on the Mac. The idea is that, no matter how far you plan ahead, you can never be totally certain if other factors

Here you can see that an entirely new column has been added.

might need to be added. In this example we have had to add a new column for the students' grades; select it by dragging right down to the bottom of the register and repeat the procedure used above for creating Borders. Notice an outline border encompasses the entire selected area.

109

Spreadsheets

Untitled 1 (SS)

B1 × ✓ Science

	A	B	C	D	E	F	
1							
2		17/12/93	15/3/94	12/6/94	1/9/94	2/9/94	Tota
3		Assignment 1	Assignment 2	Assignment 3	Assignment 4	Written Test	
4	Arthur Anderson						
5	Bart Bacharach						
6	Ché Chesney						
7	Darren Dreen						
8	Eduardo Estrada						
9	Fulton Foster						
10	Gabriel Garcia						
	Herbert						

100

Untitled 1 (SS)

B1 × ✓ Science

	A	B	C	D	E	F	
1			Science				
2		17/12/93	15/3/94	12/6/94	1/9/94	2/9/94	Total
3		Assignment 1	Assignment 2	Assignment 3	Assignment 4	Written Test	
4	Arthur Anderson						
5	Bart Bacharach						
6	Ché Chesney						
7	Darren Dreen						
8	Eduardo Estrada						
9	Fulton Foster						
10	Gabriel Garcia						
	Herbert						

A spreadsheet is merely a clean electronic piece of 'paper' waiting for your figures and calculations. We've moved from a basic shell to the rather more business-like sheet you see above. Now we are going to name it – in this case it refers to a general Science class – in a way that will look impressive in the final print-out.

To finish off the spreadsheet before we start entering data, a subject heading must be placed at the top of the chart. Resize Row 1 by moving the cursor to the left margin again and dragging the base line of Row 1 down about an inch.

Select all seven cells that will make up the heading, type a curriculum category and then resize and reformat it in the usual way. You may have to add a few judicious spaces before and after the heading if you want to eliminate the grid lines.

Once you are happy with the rough layout of the spreadsheet, you should save your work. Select Save As from the File menu and the Save As dialog box will appear. Type in a name for your document. Choose something obvious like Class 3B Annual Report. Make sure the Save As dialog box is set to Documents and click Save. Once the basic design is in place you can copy and paste it any number of times to extend the

spreadsheet to encompass other subjects on the curriculum.

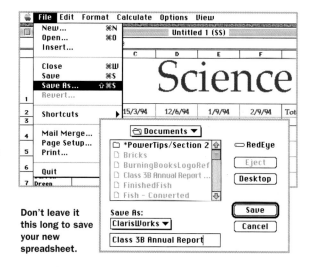

Don't leave it this long to save your new spreadsheet.

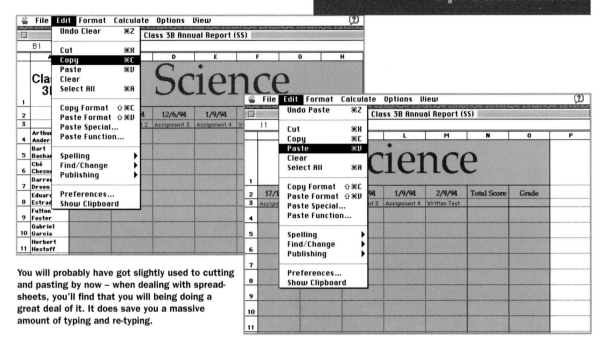

You will probably have got slightly used to cutting and pasting by now – when dealing with spreadsheets, you'll find that you will being doing a great deal of it. It does save you a massive amount of typing and re-typing.

To copy a range of cells, select it in the usual way and then choose Copy from the Edit menu (the keyboard shortcut is Command-C). In this example we have selected the entire spreadsheet apart from the first column which contains the register of names because we have assumed that all curriculum areas apply to all of the students.

After you paste the cell range to a new range of cells (notice the different cell addresses – entries – in the

pictures above), the spreadsheet may become too big for the screen. To see your whole spreadsheet at a glance, click the Zoom Out button at the bottom left-hand corner of the screen (the one with the small mountains icon).

It is now a relatively simple matter to edit the right-hand section. Select the heading in the second section and edit its contents and colour in the manner we have discussed earlier in this chapter.

The text is difficult to read for a very good reason: we have zoomed out a distance to get an overall view of the entire sheet.

Spreadsheets

Navigating your way round the document when it is displayed at full size can become quite a problem as you keep adding sections, so most spreadsheets provide a Split-Window tool that allows you to bisect the window horizontally or vertically and to scroll the sections separately. In the picture below, for example, the window has been split just to the right of Row 1 so that the students' names are always displayed in the left-hand window while you scroll through the subject areas on the right.

To split the screen, click on the thick black bar between the Zoom icons and the scroll bar and drag the tool to where you want the split to occur. To reunite your screen, click on the partition and drag it to the left or the top of the window.

You can even split the screen to compare and review data.

It is now time to start entering some figures.

To enter data in a column, follow each entry with a Return. Hitting Return confirms the entry and moves the cursor down to the next cell. (Press Tab when you are working your way across a spreadsheet and the cursor automatically moves one cell to the right.)

You don't type into a cell; look at the '83' at the top of the screen.

Select the entire cell range set aside for result and reformat in the usual way until you are happy with the way the information is presented. Reformatted empty cells will take on the appropriate attributes when you enter data.

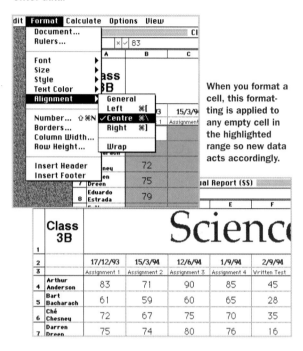

When you format a cell, this formatting is applied to any empty cell in the highlighted range so new data acts accordingly.

Here comes the supposedly tricky bit. In the Total Score column, we want to add a formula that works out the final mark for each student, taking into account the different weightings of the term-time assignments and the final written test. In the example the percentage sum of all the assignments is in weight to the percentage scored in the final test, which is marked out of 50. The formula in the Entry bar may look complicated but

Now for the formulæ – the raison d'être for spreadsheeting.

it's actually built up of very simple parts. The inner bracket is the average of the four term-time assignments. You can add cells to a formula by typing in the Entry bar or by clicking on each cell in turn. The program automatically appends a plus sign between cells that you click on:

$$(B4 + C4 + D4 + E4)/4$$

The right-hand term multiplies the written test result by two to make it a into a percentage. Remember that the test marks are out of 50:

$$(2*F4)$$

Because the percentage mark in the written test carries the same weight as all the term-time assignments together, we now add the average assignment percentage to the written test written test percentage:

$$(((B4+C4+D4+E4)/4)*(2*F4))$$

… and divide the whole thing by two:

$$=(((B4+C4+D4+E4)/4)+(2*F4))/2$$

The equals sign is required to tell *ClarisWorks* that the entry is a formula and that the result of the calculation, rather than the entry, should be pasted into the selected cell. Click the tick box and the result appears as if by magic in the cell G4.

	Class 3B Annual Report (SS)					
G4 ×√ =(((B4+C4+D4+E4)/4)+(2*F4))/2						
A	B	C	D	E	F	G
Class 3B		*Science*				
	17/12/93	15/3/94	12/6/94	1/9/94	2/9/94	Total Score
	Assignment 1	Assignment 2	Assignment 3	Assignment 4	Written Test	
Arthur Anderson	83	71	90	85	45	86.125

Once you've got the knack, formulæ become essential tools.

After the tricky bit comes the clever bit. The formula you have just created can now be copied and pasted into another cell. You might logically think that this would return the same value of 86.125 to the new cell, but because spreadsheets work by relative rather than absolute referencing this is not the case.

	Class 3B Annual Report (SS)					
G5 ×√ =(((B5+C5+D5+E5)/4)+(2*F5))/2						
A	B	C	D	E	F	G
Class 3B		*Science*				
	17/12/93	15/3/94	12/6/94	1/9/94	2/9/94	Total Score
	Assignment 1	Assignment 2	Assignment 3	Assignment 4	Written Test	
Arthur Anderson	83	71	90	85	45	86.125
Bart Bacharach	61	59	60	65	28	58.625
Ché Chesney	72	67	75	70	35	

You can re-apply equations and formulæ where you need them.

In the spreadsheet below, for example, the formula refers to its component cells in terms of how many rows and columns they are away from the selected cell, even though it contains references to specific cells. Notice it has returned the correct score of 58.625 in the second row. To paste the function into the whole column, select the column by clicking and dragging and select paste, or alternatively select Fill Down from the Calculate menu.

	Class 3B Annual Report (SS)					
G12 ×√ =(((B12+C12+D12+E12)/4)+(2*F12))/2						
A	B	C	D	E	F	
Class 3B		*Science*				
	17/12/93	15/3/94	12/6/94	1/9/94	2/9/94	Tot
	Assignment 1	Assignment 2	Assignment 3	Assignment 4	Written Test	
Arthur Anderson	83	71	90	85	45	86
Bart Bacharach	61	59	60	65	28	58
Ché Chesney	72	67	75	70	35	7
Darren Dreen	75	74	80	76	16	54
Eduardo Estrada	79	62	75	72	35	
Fulton Foster	94	82	89	95	49	
Gabriel Garcia	65	55	69	63	30	6
Herbert Hestoff	21	30	5	7	16	23
Inés Iquano	73	60	67	61	33	65

You don't have to re-type formulæ, just paste them in.

In the same way we can paste the formula into the Total Score column of other sections of the spreadsheet, as long as the same weightings apply.

	Class 3B Annual Report (SS)					
4+J4+K4+L4)/4)+(2*M4))/2						
H	I	J	K	L	M	N
			English			
rade	17/12/93	15/3/94	12/6/94	1/9/94	2/9/94	Total Score
	Assignment 1	Assignment 2	Assignment 3	Assignment 4	Written Test	
	76	73	64	59	35	69

Forward plan, and save your formulæ for other sheets as well.

If you want the numbers in the score column to be rounded up to the nearest percent, select Number from the Format menu to change the precision. Select Fixed Precision from the dialog box that appears and set the number of decimal places to 0.

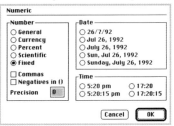

113

The totals now appear as integer numbers. You can embolden them for more emphasis by selecting Style from the Format menu in the usual way.

Format Calculate Options View

| Document... | |
| Rulers... | ual Report (SS) |

Font ▶	E	F	G
Size ▶			
Style	**Plain Text** ⌘T	
Text Color	✓**Bold** ⌘B	
Alignment	*Italic* ⌘I	
	Underline ⌘U	
Number... ⇧⌘N	S̶t̶r̶i̶k̶e̶ ̶T̶h̶r̶u̶	
Borders...	Outline	
Column Width...	Shadow	
Row Height...	Condense	
	Extend	
Insert Header		
Insert Footer	Define Styles...	

				Total Score
		'94		
		rest		
				86
				59
				70
74	80	76	16	54
62	75	72	35	71
82	89	95	49	94
55	69	63	30	62
30	5	7	16	24
60	67	61	33	66

Remember that you will want to read the answers created by your sheet on paper as well as on screen. Making totals stand out is a great help in this case.

At this stage you may also want to add formulæ to cells at the bottom of the spreadsheet to calculate the average mark for each assignment, allowing the difficulty of each assignment to be gauged and the relative performance of each student assessed against the average.

Class 3B Annual Repo

A13	✗ ✓	Average Score per Assignment		
	A	**B**	**C**	**D**	**E**
1	**Class 3B**		Scie		
2		17/12/93	15/3/94	12/6/94	1/9/
3		Assignment 1	Assignment 2	Assignment 3	Assignme
4	Arthur Anderson	83	71	90	85
5	Bart Bacharach	61	59	60	65
6	Ché Chesney	72	67	75	70
7	Darren Dreen	75	74	80	76
8	Eduardo Estrada	79	62	75	72
9	Fulton Foster	94	82	89	95
10	Gabriel Garcia	65	55	69	63
11	Herbert Hestoff	21	30	5	7
12	Inès Iquano	73	60	67	61
13	Average Score per Assignment	69	62	68	66

Calculating averages is a piece of cake once you've got the notion of formulæ under your belt. Just keep throwing data at the equation!

As well as keying in functions, *ClarisWorks* provides a library of around 100 functions that can be pasted directly to the entry bar from a dialog box.

To access the dialog box, select Paste Function from the Edit menu and click on the function you require. The function is pasted straight to the Entry bar.

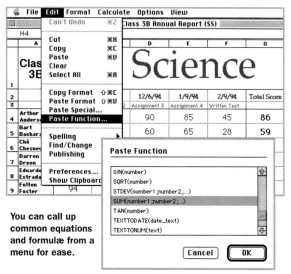

You can call up common equations and formulæ from a menu for ease.

You have to enter the arguments for the function yourself. Arguments are the fields (they can be text, number, logical proposition, or cell address) on which the outcome of the function depends. The SUM function featured, for example, requires you to fill in the brackets with a range of cell values. To enter a cell range, either type in the cell addresses you want to add or just drag the cursor from the first cell to the last. The function pastes the cell range in a shorthand notation of the form:

$$(B4..F4)$$

where all the cells from B4 through to F4 have been selected.

Edit Format Calculate Options View

			Class 3B Annual Report (SS)		
H4	✗ ✓	=SUM(B4..F4)			
	A	**B**	**C**	**D**	**E**	**F**
1	**Class 3B**					
2		17/12/93	15/3/94	12/6/94	1/9/94	2/9/94	Tot
3		Assignment 1	Assignment 2	Assignment 3	Assignment 4	Written Test	
4	Arthur Anderson	83	71	90	85	45	

Adding a number of cells together is a straightforward action.

Logical functions like IF work in pretty much the same way. You add the proposition, for example IF(G4>F4; 'Big'; 'Small') followed by the value you want *ClarisWorks* to return if the statement is true and the value (or number or cell address) you would like returned if the statement is false. All statements are listed in alphabetical order so it should be fairly straightforward to find them in the Paste Function dialog.

We are now almost ready for one of the most interesting and useful features of a spreadsheet – the ability to turn spreadsheet data into charts and graphs. We are going to need some graphics tools to edit the charts, so before you start, click on the Show Tools icon pictured at the bottom right of the image below, or select Show Tools from the View menu.

In the example below we have selected the row of figures that show Arthur Anderson's performance in the four term-time assignments. The selection area also includes the assignment names. Click on Make Chart in the Options menu.

Paste Function

FV(rate;nper;pmt;pv;type)	
HLOOKUP(lookup_value;compare_range;index)	
HOUR(serial_number)	
IF(logical;true_value;false_value)	
INDEX(range;row;column)	
INT(number)	
IRR(range;guess)	

Cancel   OK

Logical qualifiers make for extremely powerful entries.

Now your basic spreadsheet is nearing completion, you may want to experiment with different ways of displaying it and printing it out. Select Display from the Options menu and in the dialog box click the radio buttons to select the display options you require.

Options View
Make Chart...   ⌘M

Protect Cells   ⌘H
Unprotect Cells ⇧⌘H

Add Page Break
Remove Page Break
Remove All Breaks

Lock Title Position
Print Range...
Default Font...
Display...

Display

☐ Cell grid   ☒ Column headings
☐ Solid lines   ☒ Row headings
☐ Formulas   ☒ Mark circular refs

Cancel   OK

The following pictures show the spreadsheet first without the cell grid, and then with no Row or Column numbers showing.

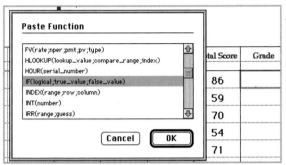

Options View
Make Chart...   ⌘M

Protect Cells   ⌘H
Unprotect Cells ⇧⌘H

Add Page Break
Remove Page Break
Remove All Breaks

Lock Title Position
Print Range...
Default Font...
Display...

Go To Cell...   ⌘G

Be careful with this menu – use all the sub-items it holds.

The next thing you see will be Chart Gallery. This menu is not Claris' finest hour. You'll use this dialog to edit almost everything about the charts you create, and they all have to be set up in advance. Don't hit OK until you have been through all the sub menus and set the chart parameters up exactly as you want them.

H14

	A	B	C	D	E	F	G
	Class 3B			**Science**			
		17/12/93	15/3/94	12/6/94	1/9/94	2/9/94	Total Sc
		Assignment 1	Assignment 2	Assignment 3	Assignment 4	Written Test	
Arthur Anderson		83	71	90	85	45	86
Bart Bacharach		61	59	60	65	28	59
Ché Chesney		72	67	75	70	35	70
Darren Dreen		75	74	80	76	16	54
Eduardo Estrada		79	62	75	72	35	71
Fulton Foster		94	82	89	95	49	94
Gabriel Garcia		65	55	69	63	30	62
Herbert Hestoff		21	30	5	7	16	24
Inès		73	60	67	61	33	66

You don't need to show the formatting when printing out.

Class 3B Annual Report (SS)

H14

Class 3B			**Science**			
	17/12/93	15/3/94	12/6/94	1/9/94	2/9/94	Total Sc
	Assignment 1	Assignment 2	Assignment 3	Assignment 4	Written Test	
Arthur Anderson	83	71	90	85	45	86
Bart Bacharach	61	59	60	65	28	59
Ché Chesney	72	67	75	70	35	70
Darren Dreen	75	74	80	76	16	54
Eduardo Estrada	79	62	75	72	35	71
Fulton Foster	94	82	89	95	49	94
Gabriel Garcia	65	55	69	63	30	62
Herbert Hestoff	21	30	5	7	16	24
Inès						

The paper presentation of spreadsheets should be simple.

There are a few other features in this dialog that are not as intuitive as they might be. However, if you take things slowly and patiently, and you follow the instructions carefully, nothing should go wrong.

Make sure not to flit around; start at the top and work your way down. The dialog you are in now is the Gallery sub menu. Notice it is greyed out in the Modify box to the left.

Click on the Bar chart icon and then click on the Axis button. Do not hit OK just yet.

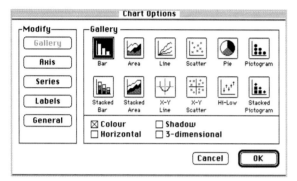

Presenting your data graphically gives a professional twist.

The fact that *ClarisWorks* comes with the capability to produce graphic representations of your data enables you to produce stunning looking charts and graphs.

As you can see from the screenshot above, the range of options open to you is, at first at least, quite intimidating. You can choose from flat pie, bar and line graphing all the way up to three dimensional representations in full-colour (if you have the equipment to output in colour that is). Take you time over these choices; you want to present the best possible image. In the Axis dialog box, you can enter headings for axes and scale increments. For the moment leave it as it is and click Series.

This shows the nuts and bolts of your charting glories.

The box with all the buttons, that looks like a terminal block, is actually for determining where the cell value is placed, if at all, inside the bar of the bar chart (or the slices of a pie chart – it all depends what chart type you chose in the gallery box). Click on the top centre button and a number 7 appears in a corresponding position in the sample box to the right. Then click Labels.

In the Labels dialog, type in a Label, Class 3B for example, and click on the block to position the label above the chart and the legend below. Then click on the General button.

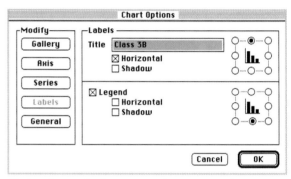

The bar-chart option is a good, solid start to graphical data.

The General dialog indicates the cell range you have selected, and lists the names of the series that will be plotted and displayed.

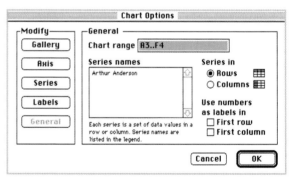

You don't need to show the entire sheet, just a range of data.

Click OK and *ClarisWorks* will draw your chart slap bang in the middle of the spreadsheet. But this is not the end of the story by any means: for a start, you don't want the graph in the middle of your sheet – all that hard work previously should be made use of. Secondly, you will probably need to make modifications to your chart in order to produce the maximum impact from all the facts and figures that you have accumulated.

To move the chart click on it and just drag it to an uncluttered part of the spreadsheet screen. Click on the label or the legend and you can edit them in the same way as you edited the cell entries themselves.

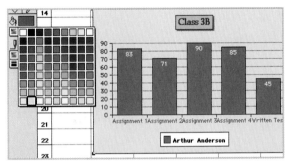

Start improving your chart with some jazzy-looking text.

You can also edit the background colour of a selected item or of the selected chart itself.

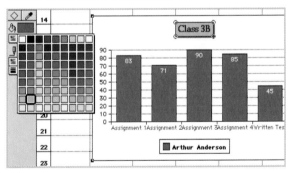

Then give additional impact by getting rid of that dull-white background (be careful if you are printing out in monochrome).

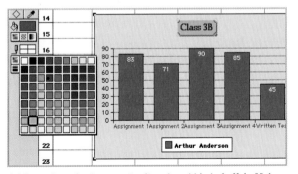

Adding colours is always a 'try it and see' kind of affair. Make sure you're not sacrificing information for pure visuals.

Change the colour of an outline by selecting the line and clicking the Pen Colour icon. (See chapter 8 – Paint Works – for the full lowdown on working with *ClarisWorks* colour editing tools).

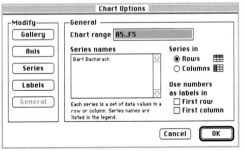

Keylines are excellent ways of making information stand out.

To modify the parameters of the chart, double click on it or select Modify Chart from the Options menu.

You can alter the range of cells (and data) for your chart.

Double clicking in white space in the chart takes you immediately back to the gallery dialog box. From here click on General and then type in a new cell range in the Chart Range field. Typing Bart Bacharach's cell range A5–F5 immediately redraws the chart with Bart's data substituted for Arthur's; a real time-saver.

Produce charts for whatever range of data you require.

117

Return to the Gallery dialog by clicking on the Gallery button or double clicking on the chart, and select Pie chart. The range of values we typed into the Chart range field correspond this time to the cells which show the average marks per assignment. The pie chart it produces gives an at-a-glance breakdown of the relative difficulty of the four assignments.

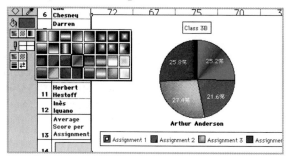

For at-a-glance value, the pie-chart takes some beating.

By clicking on the colour squares in the legend, and selecting fills or gradients from the colour fill palettes, it is possible to create some striking pie charts. The next example shows a scatter chart, created by clicking the Scatter chart icon in the Gallery dialog. The picture shows the lines of the chart being selected and edited using the Pen Size and Pen colour tools.

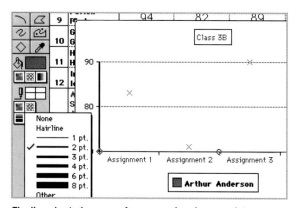

The line chart gives an unfussy way of seeing your data.

If you choose Pictogram from the Gallery dialog you can have a lot of fun with the pictures you use to build up the chart. The pictures below show a pictogram image being pasted from the Clipboard to the Pictogram sample area (see Chapter 8 for a detailed explanation of painting and drawing images).

To paste an image, select pictogram from the Gallery dialog, click on the sample box in the Series dialog, and select paste from the Edit menu. The current contents of the Mac's clipboard will be pasted into the sample box.

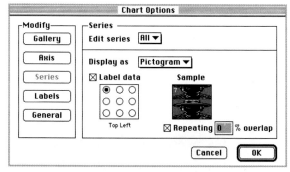

Paste your favourite image to produce the perfect pictogram.

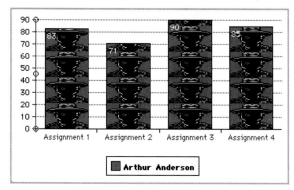

As you can see, a pictogram gives a distinct lift to dry data.

Once you are happy with your spreadsheet and your charts, you will at some stage want to print them out. First you must set the print range. This is the range of the cells that you want to print. Select Print Range from the Options menu and enter a range of cells or select the 'All cells with data' option from the dialog box.

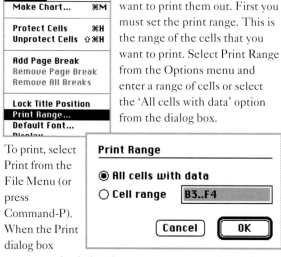

To print, select Print from the File Menu (or press Command-P). When the Print dialog box comes up, check that the parameters match those of the file you are outputting and click OK.

Multimedia

11

Multimedia playing with sound and vision it's **young technology**

Play Me

Play Me

Mac multimedia covers a wide range of applications from video conferencing and editing to animation. Developing a content-based CD-ROM is multimedia, but so is browsing or playing the results of these CD developments. You can be a multimedia consumer or a multimedia creator using authoring or playing technology...

This chapter explains how to build documents that include sound, voice and moving images, as well as the static text and graphics of traditional Mac documents.

There are two ways to go about multimedia production. One is to spend large amounts of money. The other is simply to have a go. Multimedia is a young technology. You can do what you like with it. At the heart of multimedia on Apple Mac computers is QuickTime, an extension to the Mac operating system which handles dynamic media including video, sound and animation. QuickTime can interface with other applications so multimedia hardware and software works together. QuickTime also handles compression – Apple's own and others. This is essential given the file sizes generated by simple multimedia work. The QuickTime file format is called a 'Movie', and most multimedia applications now support this format.

What You Need

Apple has two AV Macs designed to run multimedia. They're great if that's what you do most of the time, but you can create a QuickTime movie and do something useful with it on any Mac equipped with QuickTime. If you want to shoot your own video you need a video

camera, and a VCR to play the resulting video. You will also need a digitizing card if you want to capture your own video and put it on the Mac. Then comes a video editing program to enable you to exploit the flexible editing digitization provides. Finally, you may want to invest in a presentation program so you can show your movies as part of a broader presentation.

If all of that sounds far, far too expensive at the moment, there are cheaper routes: many companies are now producing dynamic clip art – copyright-free QuickTime movies on CD-ROM or disk that you can do what you like with.

Microsoft *Word* and *ClarisWorks* can both handle QuickTime. Whatever level you choose to start from, the basic processes are the same.

We wanted to show off a little, so we opted for a medium-end approach which may at present be out of reach to many readers.

However, if you get hooked on the idea and the practice of multimedia, the initial investment could be worth your while. We used a Radius VideoVision card to capture some video we had already shot, Adobe *Premiere* 3.0 to create and edit a QuickTime Movie, and *Astound*, a presentation package from Gold Disk, to create a presentation in which we embedded the movie.

▣ Video Grab

The first stage is capturing your video onto the Mac. This process involves transforming the signal on the video from analog to digital – the same difference essentially that exists between vinyl records and CDs.

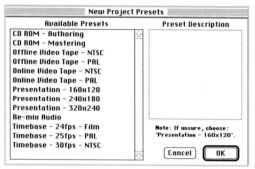

Capturing video signals entails setting up your board...

Here a Radius VideoVision board was installed to capture a movie we shot earlier from a Sony deck onto a Mac Quadra with large amounts of RAM. *Premiere*, a video editing program from Adobe was used to control the capture.

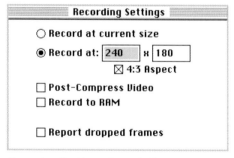

Tell your software which drive to look to...

Multimedia is greedy. You can tell *Premiere* to work with the largest space available to you by allocating a different scratch disk (a scratch disk is space-storing temporary files used by the program during its operations). Here we used a good fat 800Mb Micronet external drive for all the operations. If you're short on space clear out your hard drive before you start.

You should also set your Mac and monitor controls to handle as high a quality of colour as they are capable of. Use 24-bit colour (millions of colours) if you have it. To reset your colours or check settings, open Monitors under the Control Panels in the Apple Menu. Choose millions. Connect your video. Launch *Premiere*. Once you're in, Click Movie Capture under Capture in the File Menu and you'll see the video playing on your screen. At this point it's not being digitized but is simply playing through your screen as though it were a TV.

This helps you define the right type of video input before you begin to capture itself. We have used S-Video2 in the input channel.

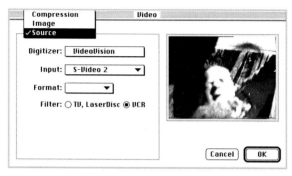

Don't forget to tell the Mac where your signal is coming from.

You also need to define the size of image you are going to capture. Here we used 240 x 180 – about a quarter of the screen size on a 14in screen.

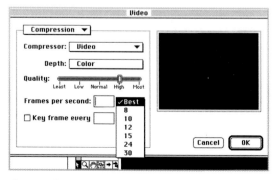

Remember, the bigger the grab, the more memory you need.

In the same window, you also need to set the right frame rate, image quality and compression – the aim is to play off the quality of the video against the available space and power of your system and hardware. The number of frames determines how smooth your captured video will be; the amount of compression determines its quality with the play off being the size of your file.

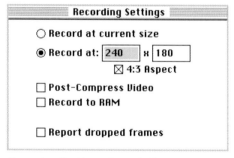

The more frames you can capture, the smoother your movie is.

Hit record and you're ready to capture the video footage you require.

When the settings have been adjusted you're ready to capture. Find the section of the video you want to use by scanning through your video using the play, rewind and fast forward controls on your VCR in the normal way. Then start the screen capture by hitting the Record button above the video screen on your Mac.

Use small clips – no more than about 15 seconds long – that way your file sizes, and your edits, will be more manageable.

To stop recording click the mouse again. Your clip will appear as a QuickTime movie. The controls at the bottom left allow you to start, stop, play, and search through it. You can play it straight away to see if you caught the required extracts.

Save all the clips needed for the project into clearly marked files.

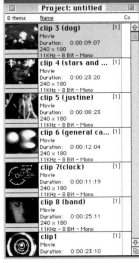

The projects soon stack up.

When enough movies have been captured, open a Project window (under the New Project sub menu in File) and drag the clips in by the top menu bars – they'll appear inside the window with useful labels indicating the size of the image (in pixels, here 240 x 180). If you closed (and saved, of course) the clips as you captured them you can Import them into the Project window (use the Import command under File menu).

If you want to capture sound separately you also need to grab some sound clips. Find the right place on your video (or other source), then use Audio Capture under Capture in the File menu.

Multimedia means making use of sound and vision. Make sure to source your audio from non-copyright areas.

Once you're happy with the level of your audio, start recording in the same way. Sound clips look like this. They can be longer than image clips but are a great deal smaller so so are less likely to cause storage problems. Drag or Import the finished sound clips into the Project window alongside the video clips. That's it; you now have a library of sound and video clips grabbed and waiting to be used. Save your Project and give it a name.

Don't save your work with the weird names – it'll make your life difficult in the long run.

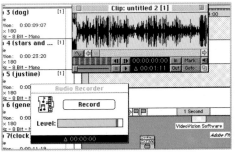

Recording audio is more straightforward than it looks.

121

How To Edit your Movie

Video editing programs such as *Premiere* or *VideoShop* enable different clips of film to be combined together smoothly. You can also add text such as screen titles, and you can also introduce a wide range of special effects and transitions. It's here you have the chance to get creative and add impact to grabbed video or a pre-existing QuickTime clip.

Start back at the Project window. Make sure all the clips you've recorded are Imported into this window. Then turn to the Construction window. This consists of two video tracks, the Video A or B channels, an Audio A and B channel, and two tracks for special effects and transitions. The tracks are arranged along a time line.

Physically pick up and drag your first clip of film and place it at the start of the Construction window. Put it into Channel A. If you recorded sound alongside the video signal, you'll see sound coming in along the bottom line (if you don't want this, select it by clicking and kill it by deleting). Add some more clips onto the top Channel A if you want the film to run together. Put other clips onto Channel B if you want to create some transition effects between them later.

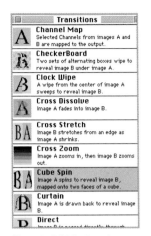

Transitions	
Channel Map	Selected Channels from images A and B are mapped to the output.
CheckerBoard	Two sets of alternating boxes wipe to reveal image B under image A.
Clock Wipe	A wipe from the center of image A sweeps to reveal image B.
Cross Dissolve	Image A fades into image B.
Cross Stretch	Image B stretches from an edge as image A shrinks.
Cross Zoom	Image A zooms in, then image B zooms out.
Cube Spin	Image A spins to reveal image B, mapped onto two faces of a cube.
Curtain	Image A is drawn back to reveal image B.
Direct	Image B is passed directly through

Transitions	
Displace	The red and green channels of image A displace the pixels of image B.
Dither Dissolve	Image A Dissolves into image B.
Doors	Image B swings in over image A on horizontal or vertical doors.
Fold Up	Image A is repeatedly folded over to reveal image B.
Funnel	Image A is pulled through a funnel, revealing image B.
Inset	A corner wipe reveals image B under image A.
Iris Cross	A cross shaped wipe opens to reveal image B under image A.
Iris Diamond	A diamond shaped wipe opens to reveal image B under image A.
Iris Points	A pointed wipe closes to reveal image

Your straight footage is now ready to be played around with.

drag the icon you choose from the Transitions window across to the Construction window and place it between the two clips you want to link in the T (Transitions) channel. Clicking turns the pointer into a crosshead and you can adjust the length of the transition by dragging it out.

You can edit the Transitions by double clicking on the icon representing the effect being put in place. Here, using Cube Spin (it puts the pictures into a die and slowly rotates), it was possible to set the start and end points and the angle of rotation. It was also easy to kill the border or edit its colour.

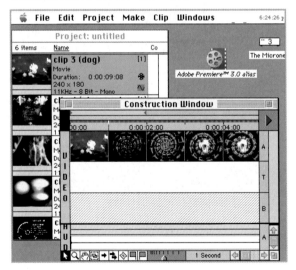

Each of the clips become parts of a single 'construction'.

The Transitions menu has a wide range of effects, from the traditional cross-fade – one image dissolves into the next – to dithers, funnels, fold-ups, wipes and more. As soon as you select the windows, the icons come alive to demonstrate the effects they create. To create a transition

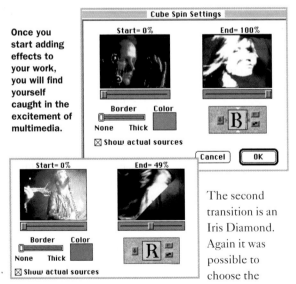

Once you start adding effects to your work, you will find yourself caught in the excitement of multimedia.

The second transition is an Iris Diamond. Again it was possible to choose the direction of the effect and set entry and exit points. Once the effect has been placed in your movie you can see how the transition will work in slow motion by clicking on Sources.

A different way to add effects is to superimpose one clip on top of another and make it more or less transparent. Here a somewhat Doctor Who-like time tunnel was placed in the superimpose channel ready to appear over the singer.

Once the clips are in place choose Transparency.

under the Clip menu. Effectively we filtered out all the information in the top slide except the edges of the rings. These then sit on top of the singer. Viewing the sample means it's possible to experiment until you achieve the desired effect.

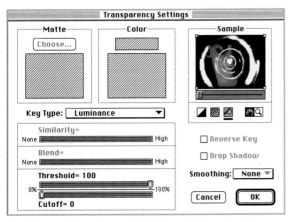

There's no point having an effect if you can't see the film.

You may want to add some titles. Here we included a Dog Rated logo from the dog in the movie clips. Select New Title from the File menu. Type in your text and edit the font, style and colour – you could easily add drop shadows too. *Premiere* will handle any PostScript font. Once you've created a title, Save it and Import it back into your Project.

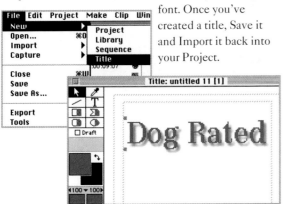

You still need to use the written word to explain a few points.

Power*Tips*........

⚡ **STAR WITH THE BEST: use as high a quality original as you can. Our video is S-VHS. The better the quality you start with, the better your finished work. Inevitably the process involves some degradation of the image.**

⚡ **SPEEDY TIP: if you place all your clips in a single folder as you capture them, you can Import them into the Project window in one speedy move instead of having to import them file by file.**

⚡ **FRAME RATE: Frame Rate determines how smoothly your movie will run. It is in turn determined by how much you spend on your digitizing card. The standard frame rates for video and film will fall between 24 and 30 frames per second. Some lower cost capture cards can only handle around 15. This will give you serviceable movies, but don't expect wide-screen, blockbuster quality.**

⚡ **MORE MEMORY: it may be tempting to view your clips frame by frame but it will make your Construction window too large, long and slow. Use the view tool at the bottom of the window to set reasonable intervals. Trade off the flexibility this gives you getting around the window against the detail you can see in the clips – and use the Preview tool for localized editing.**

⚡ **FRAME-BY-FRAME: If your program runs out of memory, you can allocate more by applying the Get Info (Command-I or Get Info under the File menu in the Finder).**

Then increase the amount of memory above the recommended level – which will be in the 'Suggested' box. Experiment to see how far you can usefully push this up. Take backups while experimenting. Remember you can't do this with an Alias. You must have the original application.

Multimedia

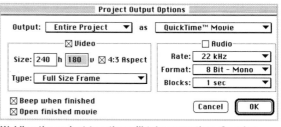

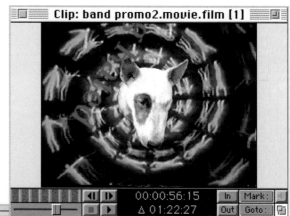

This is multimedia, so of course you can animate your text.

Titles can be given Motion Settings. Here our Dog Rated label has been set to rotate 360° while zooming in from the top left to bottom right of the screen. You can view the effect in the smaller box and edit by dragging the lines in the larger one. Finally drag it onto the Superimpose channel of the Construction window. (You will also want to make sure the white background is transparent – use the Transparency controls to do this, in the same way as before.)

The Construction window takes shape. To preview different bits of film, use the yellow preview marker above the channels. This gives you a frame by frame run through and you can check how transitions are working. To add independent sound drag it onto the construction window from the Project Window. You can adjust the length in the same way as for video. It is also possible to use Looped sound – that is sound that runs back into

itself and will keep going indefinitely.

When you're happy with your clip save it as a QuickTime Movie. Select the Movie command under the Make menu. Choosing QuickTime allows you to control the frame rate, compression and the audio settings. Make some coffee while your movie is being created… Then make some more coffee.

Welding the project together will take some time. So relax.

It can take some time. Finally play the movie through, and enroll for film school.

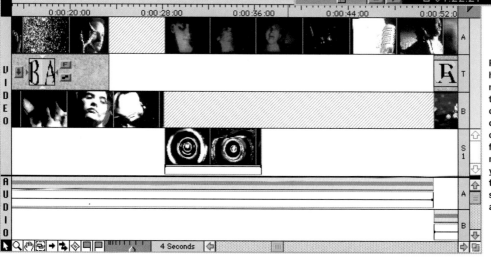

Producing high-quality work means attention to detail. In this case you can check your project on a frame-by-frame basis to make certain that you are achieving the flow and the styling that you are aiming for.

24

HOW TO Embed a Movie

You can use your movie on its own, but movies can also be embedded in other documents to add impact to any message. Here we used *Astound*, a presentation package from Gold Disk to show how you can put QuickTime into a multimedia 'slide' to build up a multimedia presentation to be played back on a Mac. There are a number of other packages, for example Aldus *Persuasion*, which could equally well be used.

Open *Astound* and choose New Presentation. This pulls you straight into the first slide. On the left a range of tools provide quick ways to insert the different types of objects (including lines, text and drawings, but also animated objects, graphics and QuickTime movies) that will make up the slides. Typing in text is straightforward.

Text is a powerful tool, it's also not too heavy on your system.

The original backdrop selected was solid blue, but a gradient colour could be added. Once the Gradient tool has been selected, it's possible to tailor the direction and intensity of the gradient used and blend the colours. Choose New Slides either under the Slide command in the menu bar or hit the New Slide button on the bottom left of the window.

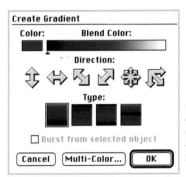

Blends of hues (called Gradients) have as much impact if used as backgrounds as do primary washes.

Add some still images if you want to include them. Here an image from the original QuickTime movie was exported as a PICT file and then re-imported into Astound. To Import a PICT click on the image icon (the mountains and sun picture) and cycle through your files. Select the one you need.

Don't forget the power of a good static image in your work.

Add your QuickTime movie by clicking the QuickTime icon – then drag out a place for the movie on your slide screen, find the movie you want, and click OK. The Insert command can also be used. In this case the movie will appear at the size you created it. To check out the movie once it's placed, hit the Slide button at the bottom of the screen on the right and you can watch the movie play. Double clicking on the movie brings up the QuickTime surround, and different in and out points can be set.

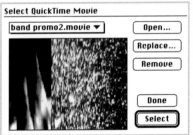

Watch your movie in preview form before deciding to inflict it on the rest of the the un-multimedia aware world. Does fame beckon to you?

Add different shapes or graphics using the tools within the program. Here stars were used to link two pictures and surrounding text on slide number 4.

Simple multimedia can still be effective...

You can also add buttons to slides. These enable you to assign a certain action, triggered by pressing the button – for example a sound could be played, or a slide could move on or move back. To create one, click the button icon, and a button will appear; you can resize it and colour it as required. Here we rough-placed three buttons to which different songs were attached.

Enable other people to play your piece by adding 'hot' buttons.

To see how your presentation is taking shape, click the slide sorter box on the left of the screen. This gives a thumbnail view of the presentation. You can alter the order of slides.

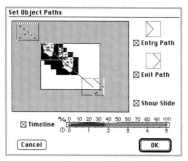

Once again, make sure to keep an eye on the work in progress.

Astound allows you to apply special effects including transitions to objects within slides and between different slides. It also allows these transitions to be precisely timed.

Here we chose to apply a transition to an object – in this case a still image taken from the band movie. You

can define an entry and exit point of the image, and the path the image will take, by dragging the visual paths within the image. The time bar below allows the length of the

It's time to forget that a static image is a static image, it's time to play with it.

transition effect on entry and exit to be prescribed by dragging the pale blue lines in and out.

Rotation can also be added. Here a star was set to appear on the slide, bounce around and move out again. Making a title move across a page is possible by selecting the text and applying different effects including fades, wipes, dissolves and different motions. You can also load different sounds. Click on the speaker icon on the side bar to load a sound and control its length, volume and input and exit points.

Once you have your elements on the page and have ascribed timings to them, use the clock tool on the right of the screen. Timing can be set for every different element making up a slide. So, for example, the title could be set to cut in early, followed by pictures, then sound.

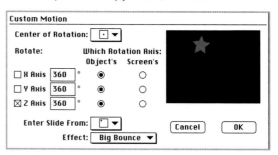

Bouncing shapes around the screen to your heart's delight.

Finally, you can set transition effects to jazz up the switch from slide to slide. When you're happy save the work as a project. Notice you can save it as a self-running version, but this doesn't include QuickTime;

Finally, save, save and save again. You must remember to look after your work.

you have to add that separately. That's it. An instant guide to multimedia. You've now captured, edited and used a movie in a presentation. This area is vast in big business, however it is growing all the time in non-commercial areas; the choice is totally up to you. A great way to start is to buy some clip media, install the latest version of QuickTime – consult your dealer, it's getting better by leaps and bounds – and try it out.

Power *Tips* •

TEXT WITH MOVIES: it is easy to add a QuickTime movie to a Word or Works document.

Open a *ClarisWorks* document in Word Processing mode. Choose Insert under the File Menu – remember to check the preview box to make sure the movie being placed is the right one.

The movie has landed. Note the QuickTime icon at the bottom of the picture. Double click on the picture or the controls to launch the movie. Here it's an inline graphic so it will move with the text placed around it.

Then add the required text, add boxes and Send to the Back. Save the result for an instant presentation.

ASTOUNDING: It's more sensible to use the Import option than to draw out a box first for your QuickTime movie in *Astound* – that way the proportions will be right and the movie should run more smoothly.

Don't make your clips too long – they're harder to edit and they'll take up valuable processing power and hard disk space.

THE ONE THAT GOT AWAY: *Premiere* involves an amazing number of files. If you lose one, use Find straightaway – Adobe has thoughtfully put this command on the Place box. And call your files something relevant.

EXPORTING SINGLE FRAMES FROM QUICKTIME MOVIES: this is easy. Run through your movie clip. Stop where you want to be. You can export your chosen screen as a PICT via the Edit menu. Recombine your still PICTs as a backdrop for your QuickTime Movie presentation as we did above. You could do the same in *Word* or *ClarisWorks* too.

127

❗ ALERT

**1 If you want to get involved in Multimedia, you are going to need RAM.
2 Save As... so you can retain the integrity of your film.**

COPYRIGHT

Be very careful. You may simply be sampling a video to make something new, but the copyright lawyers may not take the same view. If it's commercial, even public, get permission. Use copyright-free clip movies, or better still shoot your own (it's more fun).

Expanding Your Mac

12

What is SCSI?

This icon means SCSI-compatible. Look for it on the back of your Mac.

SCSI stands for Small Computer Systems Interface, and is pronounced 'scuzzy'. It's a method of connecting devices such as disk drives, CD-ROM drives and scanners to your Macintosh; some low-cost printers are also connected via the SCSI port. You can 'chain' up to six SCSI devices to your Mac by connecting one to the other (they should all have two sockets on the back to let you do this), and linking the last one to the Mac's SCSI port.

If you only have one SCSI device, connection should be fairly straightforward, as long as you follow the manufacturer's instructions carefully. However, things can get a little more tricky if you have more than one – in that case, you'll need a 'SCSI-to-SCSI lead' to connect one to the other (the cable that you normally get is a 'Mac-to-SCSI', which isn't quite the same). You also need to fit a 'terminator' to the last SCSI device in the chain. This is a small unit that plugs in to the free SCSI socket at the end of the chain, and gets the whole thing working properly. A terminator is usually supplied with any SCSI device, and the manuals should give you plenty of information on how exactly to connect things up.

When you first got your Mac you probably couldn't think of anything that needed to be added to it – it was fine as it was, and anyway, you probably spent all your budget on buying the best machine possible. As you become more experienced, however, you'll find more and more 'peripherals' start to seem appealing if not absolutely necessary to the work you find yourself becoming involved in: you're going to need a printer perhaps, or an extra hard drive to store all your work.

Then again, maybe you'll find that your Mac needs more memory to let you run two or three applications at the same time, or a larger monitor because you've found that you're doing a lot of DTP work. In this chapter we'll take a brief look at the sort of things you could add to your Mac to make it a more powerful machine.

Remember though, that new equipment is being introduced all the time – so you should keep your eye on magazines and even bulletin board systems (BBSs) to make sure that you're as up to date as possible on new developments before you pay out all your hard-earned cash on new pieces of equipment.

INTERNAL UPGRADES

There are some upgrades that you can make internally to your Mac, to improve its performance. The most popular of these is to increase the amount of RAM in the machine. This will mean that more applications can run at the same time – you swap between them as you wish, and you don't have to Quit one before you start another.

If you have a 'compact' Mac – that is, one with a built-in screen such as the Classic, Classic II, Color Classic or Performa 200, you shouldn't attempt to add more RAM yourself. Opening the machine is tricky, and can be dangerous – the screen can retain a high voltage charge for many hours after it's turned off. If you want to increase the memory in such a machine, the best thing to do is take it in to your local Apple dealer.

However, if you have a Mac with a separate monitor, upgrading the RAM is a relatively simple task, provided you are confident and careful. Most memory upgrade kits these days contain full step-by-step instructions, and the whole procedure should take less than ten minutes. Be warned, though: if you upgrade the RAM yourself you'll invalidate your warranty. If you damage your Mac in the process, you will have to foot the cost of all the repairs – so only take on the job if you're confident that you know what you're doing. Again, if you're unsure you should take the machine to an Apple dealer, who will perform the upgrade for you. As for exactly what kind of RAM you need, and how much you can add, the best advice here is to talk to a memory supplier – lots of companies sell RAM these days, probably including the place where you bought your Mac. There are many different configurations, and Apple's product line is changing rapidly, so it really is important to get up-to-date information about what kind of RAM your Mac uses before embarking on an upgrade. To find the current amount of RAM installed on your Mac, use About This Macintosh – access it from the Apple menu (make sure you're in the Finder).

PRINT POWER

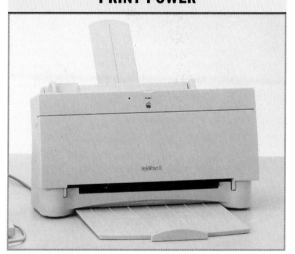

Apple's StyleWriter printers are ideal for the home user.

Probably the most popular peripheral bought by Macintosh users is a printer. After all, it's fine being able to create beautiful-looking documents on screen, but there's not much point unless you can output them and give them to someone else!

The most popular printer is the StyleWriter II. This is a 'bubblejet' printer, which means that it works by squirting tiny bubbles of ink onto the page to make up the letters and images. It's a 360 dots per inch (dpi) printer, so the kind of output quality that it produces is excellent, whether you want to print a letter to the bank or your child's latest graphics masterpiece.

If you're really serious about quality, nothing beats a laser printer. Prices are coming down all the time, and if you shop around there's every chance that you could pick up a bargain. Do, however, make sure that you buy one that's Mac-compatible – many dealers sell low-cost laser printers through adverts in newspapers, but normally they won't interface to the Mac.

To connect your laser printer, you're often told that you need an AppleTalk connector. If you're not careful, you'll be sold a full AppleTalk connection kit – which can cost $40 or more – when all that you actually need is a Macintosh serial cable (sometimes called an ImageWriter cable). This links your printer to the port on the back of the Mac identified by an icon that looks like a printer, and works perfectly well. Best of all, it only costs a quarter of the price of the full kit.

Once your printer is linked up, all you need to do is install the 'printer driver' software that came with it, select it from the Chooser (which can be found under the Apple menu) and you're ready to print away.

EXTRA STORAGE

CD-ROM is an excellent way of accessing huge amounts of data.

At some point, you may find that you're running out of space on your Mac's hard disk. If this is the case, you'll want to consider adding an extra hard disk to your set-up. These disk (they are also, confusingly, called drives) are known as external hard disks, and appear on your Desktop just like your current hard disk. You'll then be able to store documents and applications on either one.

Hard disks connect via the SCSI port, so you'll need to make sure that you get a 'Mac-to-SCSI' cable when you order the drive – most come with such a cable as standard but do double-check.

Another SCSI device is the CD-ROM drive. CD-ROM stands for Compact Disc Read-Only Memory, and is a method of storing several hundreds of megabytes of information on a disk which is just like an audio CD. You can't record data onto such a disk yourself. Well that is not strictly true; there are rewritable CDs appearing on the market as we write this book. However, the major stumbling block that stands in the way of the average Mac user is the price not only of the discs but also of the equipment you need to write to a compact disc.

You really are looking at the 1,000s rather than 100s of green folding money if you want to get into the realms of CD-ROM authoring. On top of this, you will also have needed somewhere to store the data you want to put onto your CDs. With the average compact disc holding somewhere in the region of 650Mb, this means another outlay on your part.

In reality, CD-ROM is designed for software developers to give you vast quantities of data, far more than could be shipped out on floppy disks at a reasonable price (a 650Mb CD would need more than 450 floppy disks to match its storage capacity, and the the cost of duplicating and packaging these would mean hugely expensive software).

The software developers are currently having the time of their lives with the new storage capacities offered by CD-ROM; for example, you can get entire encyclopedias and other reference works on CD-ROM. For less seriously minded people there are stunning, full-color graphic games, that include movie clips and very high quality sound, now appearing on this format.

Again, linking a CD-ROM drive to your system is simply a case of plugging it in to the SCSI port and installing the supplied software. You can use it to play audio CDs too.

FASTER FASTER

There is little or no point in adding new drives, vast amounts of RAM, CD-ROM drives and other peripherals if you're Mac starts to move at 2MPH because it is weighed down by all this new responsibility.

If you really feel that your Mac is too slow for the work that you're doing, one way to speed things up is to buy an accelerator card. This is an extra circuit board that fits inside the Macintosh and makes the whole machine work faster. These boards can more than double your Mac's original speed. A warning though, you must check with your dealer that the board you are about the pay out your money for will work with your Mac. There are many different boards for different kinds of Mac.

Power Tips.........

VIRUS ALERT: Despite popular myths, it quite possible for a CD-ROM to carry a computer virus. Don't be fooled into thinking that because CDs are read-only, that they can't be infected – remember there are occasions when you have to copy files from CD to your hard disk. DO make sure to virus check all CDs in the same way as you would check a floppy disk.

HIDDEN COSTS: Remember the hidden costs when buying a printer. If you use a StyleWriter for example, you will need to buy ink cartridges and paper. A laserwriter means toner (which is expensive) and paper. Factor these costs in to your purchase budget.

PRICE WATCH: Memory (RAM) prices vary from week-to-week (sometimes from day to day). Keep your eyes on the computer press to make sure that your dealer is not charging last week's (over-priced) RAM costs for this week's stock. RAM is one of the most fluctuating markets in the world.

SHOCKING: When adding any new hardware to you Mac, MAKE SURE that you have switched it off at the mains (take the plug out to be certain). Do not an any account plug a new drive, printer or scanner into your Mac if it is switched on. There is a chance that plugging a new cable into a 'live' Mac can cause a short-circuit that could cause expensive damage to your beloved machine. Don't take the chance. Do switch off.

EARTHY MEMORY: if you have decided to fit your own RAM upgrades to your Mac (be certain that you know that you're doing) make sure that you earth yourself before touching the new chips. Many people can build up quite an (un)healthy static charge during the course of a day – you don't want this transferring to your Mac's new memory. One the best ways to earth yourself (in order to let any charge find its way to the ground) is to touch a metal radiator. This way the static can escape via the plumbing! Sounds silly but it's quite true.

Troubleshooting Your Mac

13

What do you do when it all goes horribly wrong? Well, don't panic: most of the problems that you're likely to come across on your Mac are easy to solve. Here we'll run through some of the most common troubles, and provide simple solutions.

Q **My Macintosh tells me that there isn't enough memory to launch an application that I double-clicked on.**

A You're probably already running one or more programs on your Mac. Go to the small icon (the application menu) in the top right-hand corner of the menu bar and click on it. You'll see a menu appear which lists all the currently running applications. The Finder is always there, but if there are any others select them one at a time, which brings them to the foreground, and then select Quit from the File menu.

If you still get the message and you're not running any other applications, then you'll have to persuade the Mac to launch the program using less memory. Click once on the program's icon, and select Get Info from the Finder's File menu. This will present you with some information on the program, and at the bottom right-hand corner you'll see a field for the application's current memory size. Try reducing this by typing in a new number (don't reduce it to less than the 'minimum size' that's also displayed there) and close the Info window. Now try running the application again.

If this still doesn't work, then you really don't have enough memory to run the program, and you'll have to think about upgrading the amount of RAM that you have fitted – see Chapter 12 'Expanding your Mac'.

Q **All my fonts seem 'jagged' on the screen.**

A This means that you have installed some PostScript fonts. The Mac ships with TrueType fonts, which will appear smooth on the screen whatever size you display them at. To make PostScript fonts appear smooth, you'll have to buy a program

called *Adobe Type Manager* (often referred to as *ATM*). However, unless you're intending to do any professional publishing – for example, using a bureau – it would be better to stick to TrueType fonts anyway. There are plenty available, and they work perfectly well on all Macs running System 6.0.7 or later.

Q **I installed a new Extension or Control Panel and now my Mac 'freezes' as it starts up. I see some icons across the bottom of the screen, but then nothing happens – the normal Desktop doesn't appear.**

A You've probably got what's known as an 'Extension clash', or 'INIT clash' (Extensions used to be known as INITs before System 7). To start your Mac up, hold down the Shift key as you switch on the power. Keep Shift pressed until the 'Welcome to Macintosh' screen appears, and you should see the message 'Extensions off' appear.

This message means that you've temporarily disabled all the Extensions, so your Mac should start up as normal. Now you can remove the Extension that you just installed, because that's almost certainly the one causing the problem.

Either it isn't compatible with System 7 (possibly because it's an old piece of software) or it's 'conflicting' with another Extension that you have installed.

Unfortunately, the only way to find out which one it's conflicting with is to remove them all from the Extensions folder, which is inside the System folder, then replace them one at a time, restarting the Mac each time, until the trouble recurs. Then, the last one that you replaced is the one that's making the Mac crash. This is another good reason to keep a track of all the files on your Mac.

Q I can't print my documents to the printer.

A There are a few possible reasons for this. Let's start with the obvious ones (because these are the ones that are most often over-looked). First of all, make sure that your printer is switched on! Then check that the cable connecting the printer and the Mac is securely in place.

Remember that if you're outputting to a laser printer you'll have to wait half a minute or so for it to start up before it can accept documents for output.

Now look in the Chooser, and make sure that everything's OK there. That means selecting the printer driver icon on the left, then checking that the printer name is selected (if it's a network printer) or that you've clicked on the correct port that it's connected to (if it's a StyleWriter or similar printer). Also, check whether Background Printing is on or off – if it's on, it will take longer for the printer to output your file, so maybe you just haven't waited long enough.

Q Sometimes, when I save a file from an application and then quit, the document I've saved doesn't have the right icon – instead, it has the 'plain paper' icon.

A This means that you need to rebuild your Desktop file. The Desktop file is an invisible file that contains lots of information that the Finder needs for things such as displaying the correct icons – and sometimes it gets slightly corrupted.

This isn't really a cause for concern, since you can 'rebuild' it easily. To do so, Restart your Macintosh and hold down the Command and Option keys on the keyboard, until a dialog box appears asking you whether you really want to rebuild the Desktop. Click on Yes, and wait until the process is complete. Your icons should now be displayed correctly.

It's a good idea to rebuild your Desktop file every week or so as a matter of course – it helps avoid problems such as the one above, and can also help to keep your Mac running at top speed. Once you're more confident with your Mac you can try the following shortcut: first quit from any programs that you are running. Next hold down Option Command esc. Your Mac will ask you if you want to restart the Finder! Keep the Command and Option keys held down and click on the Okay button. The screen will blank for a moment and then you'll be asked whether you want to rebuild the Desktop. Click in Okay and off you go. It's the same process as from restart, but this time you can do it without having to switch on and switch off. If anything goes wrong – for example, you can't get rid of the Do You Want To Restart Finder – don't panic. Switch off your Mac and leave it for a few moments. Then switch it back on.

Q I threw away a file by mistake, and now I want to get it back. Is it possible?

A Not using the standard software that comes with the Mac. However, if you have a program such as *Norton Utilities for Macintosh*, *MacTools Deluxe* or *Complete Undelete* you may well be able to recover your file – as long as you do so within a couple of days of throwing it away (ideally you should do it within a few seconds!).

After this it may have been overwritten or lost. Incidentally, *Norton Utilities* is a very worthwhile package – it also contains the *Norton Disk Doctor* program, which can help to make sure that your hard disk is in good shape and is free from problems.

One thing you should try and avoid if you are going to make use of any file-recovery software, is trashing anything else after you've deleted the file you want back. Doing so will complicate the rescue software's task.

Finally, keep in mind that, just because you've put a file into the Mac's garbage receptacle doesn't mean that you have deleted it yet. Before panicking, open it up and see if you can drag your files back to the hard disk.

Q When I try to start up my Mac I get a picture of a blank disk on the screen, together with a flashing question mark, rather than the normal 'Welcome to Macintosh' picture.

A This means that the Mac can't find a System disk to boot (start up) from. The reason for this is probably because the System file on your hard disk has become corrupted, although it may mean that

132

there's a hardware problem with the disk drive. Try booting up from the emergency disk of a disk utilities package such as *Norton Utilities*, and see if that fixes the problem. This brings up the obvious tip: make sure to create a back-up System disk. LC and Quadra owners can do this using the installation software that came with their machines. If you've got a Performa, you'll have to buy a set of System disks. Having a spare floppy to boot from can save a great deal of stress and distress in the long run.

If not, try reinstalling the System using the Installer disks that came with your Mac. (Performa owners won't have had such a set of disks, and unfortunately will have to buy a copy of System 7.1 to do this.) If the Installer utility can't find the hard drive, then it's a hardware fault and you should take the Mac to your dealer for repair.

Q **When I try to start up my Mac I get a 'sad Mac' – the picture has its mouth turned down, and appears white on a black background.**

A Oh dear, you really did not want to see this one. No beating about the bush here, this is bad news. This could mean that you have a hardware fault, in which case you'll need to get a specialist to look at your Mac.

However, there could be a slightly less traumatic scenario afoot… if you've attached any SCSI devices (external disk drives, scanners, graphics tablets) to your Macintosh, you could have a SCSI problem. Unplug all of the SCSI devices from the Mac and try to restart; if everything works OK now, it was a SCSI clash and not a 'real' hardware fault.

The first thing to do is to make sure that all your SCSI devices have different ID numbers. There's normally a switch on the back of each unit to change the ID. And make sure that all the IDs are between 1 and 6. Your Mac's internal hard drive, which is also a SCSI device, should have ID number 0 – so do ensure that you have not given any of the new devices this ID number because it really will cause massive problems.

If no SCSI devices are attached and you still get the 'sad Mac', then unfortunately you may well have a hardware problem – check your warranty to see who to contact for a repair.

VIRUSES AND WHAT TO DO ABOUT THEM

There is a lot of paranoia about computer viruses, so let's get the story straight here. Viruses are files that are designed to spread without your knowledge and which may have an effect on your system or your data. You can catch viruses via files downloaded through bulletin boards, or through networked Macs or via floppy disks (especially pirated or ones 'copied from friends'). To be brutally honest, splendid isolation is your only 100 per cent solution.

Fortunately the problem does not warrant this type of extreme solution. There are only a handful of viruses that can infect your Mac, and almost none of them are intended to harm your data – normally they're just designed to spread from one application to another, and from one Mac to another. However, it is still wise to take some precautions against 'catching' a virus, and the best thing to do is get hold of a freeware utility called *DISINFECTANT.* You can get it from PD houses, bulletin boards or user groups. The great thing is that it is absolutely free – pass it on to anyone else you know with a Mac.

DISINFECTANT scans your Macintosh to make sure that it's virus free, and if it does find anything (very unlikely) it will remove it for you.

Don't be too paranoid about viruses. As long as you're sensible – don't take material from sources you aren't sure about, and make sure that you've got a program like *DISINFECTANT* – you'll be fine.

Finding Out More

14

With around 10 million Mac users around the world, you're not alone sitting there in front of a flashing screen wondering what to do next. Now you've mastered the way the Mac works and the basics of applications there's plenty of places to go for help, advice, interest and information – from bulletin boards and on-line services, where you use your telephone line to access information on other open-access computers around the world – to user groups, where like-minded people get together to discuss problems and sort out solutions.

GETTING NETWORKED

We live in a global village. Using your Mac and a modem (a device – costing anything from $100 to $900 – to link your computer to a telephone line) you can gain access to bulletin boards on other computers, anywhere in the world, often for a nominal subscription fee. Bulletin board services can provide access to information from weather reports and computer developer information, to stock prices and film reviews.

What's around?

• *Electronic Mail (Email):* Electronic mail allows you to type a message on screen and then send it to another subscriber of the bulletin board, who can be anywhere in the world. When you subscribe to a bulletin board, you are given an email address, which is either a number or a name (for example caroline@cix.Compulink.co.uk) to which people can send messages.

• *Shareware:* Bulletin boards contain thousands of shareware, freeware and public domain programs that you can download (that's to say copy legally) to your very own Macintosh.

Shareware software is distributed on a try-before-you-buy basis. If you like the software and use it, you should send money – often a nominal fee of around $10 to $15 – to the writer of the program (the fee is normally quoted in dollars even if you are registering Italian shareware!).

Freeware can be used for free, but copyright is still retained on the program by the writer.

Public domain software is completely free with no copyright restrictions. The most popular shareware and freeware programs are *Disinfectant* (a virus checker), *SCSI Probe* (a utility which allows you to mount peripheral storage devices on your Mac more easily and check SCSI

ID numbers), *StuffIt Expander* (for decompressing files downloaded from bulletin boards) and *ZTerm* (a program which enables you to communicate through your modem). All these are available on the Internet, CompuServe, GEnie, America OnLine and CIX.

• *Support:* Bulletin boards are subscribed to by all major Mac developers and manufacturers, which gives you easy access to software upgrades, product release information and technical specifications. Upgrades to most software is available on AppleLink and CompuServe in the relevant sections, and AppleLink contains technical information on all Apple equipment and for most of the third-party peripheral devices such as hard disks, monitors, scanners and modems.

There are also boards where you can post (send electronically) questions about equipment that you are having trouble with in the knowledge that there will be someone reading it who will have the answer – some of the people reading it will have written the software and developed the hardware personally.

• *Conferences:* Conferences (or forums) on bulletin boards are places where like-minded people get together. You might join a desktop publishing conference, for example, to pass messages to, and ask questions of, other people in the field.

Each conference can be broken down into specific sections, so that you could talk to people who use the same program as you. On a more serious level, you might be obsessed with the Grateful Dead and want to shoot the breeze with other Deadheads – they'll be there.

• *Information:* Bulletin boards provide massive information resources with a few clicks of the mouse. For instance, on-line CompuServe has the Academic American Encyclopedia, a complete list of books in print, access to articles in hundreds of magazines and newspapers, *Magill's Survey of Cinema*, market research reports, over 25,000 book reviews, news services and stock prices from around the world, trademark libraries, weather reports and companies information – all of it accessible at the twitch of a mouse.

GETTING FURTHER INFO

• *AppleLink:* This is Apple's worldwide bulletin board service, with all Apple developers and manufacturers. Mac interface is supplied to subscribers, but costs are high. Contact AppleLink on your local Apple number. Apple is also planning a new consumer-based bulletin board service called eWorld.

• *CompuServe:* the biggest on-line service in the world. Mac-like interface with Information Manager *CompuServe Information Manager* software, but relatively expensive. Look in you the latest edition of your preferred Mac magazine for current rates and your local log-on number.

• *The Internet:* a massive global network of thousands of computers, with links to education sites, and commercial and government users (contact Bill Clinton through his email address of president@whitehouse.gov, for instance). You will need some specialised number and a local log-on number but the Internet really really gives you global access.

GETTING ONTO APPLELINK

When you subscribe to AppleLink, you get the AppleLink software, which is the way to sign on. This has been developed so that the computer you connect with looks and feels like a Mac. You will get the local access number to ring AppleLink using your modem and you'll also need to configure the modem.

1 After installing the AppleLink software, double-click on the AppleLink icon. You will be asked to type in your password to gain access to AppleLink.

AppleLink is soon to be overtaken by Apple's eWorld, we hope!

2 AppleLink illustrates the process graphically – if problems occur you'll know where they are located.

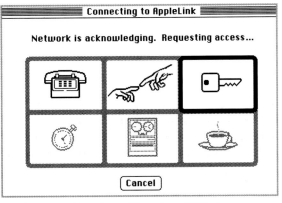

Logging on is achieved smoothly and graphically for you.

3 The In Basket is where incoming mail is stored, the Out Basket is a store of mail messages you have sent and the AppleLink Services are the conferences of which you are a member. By double-clicking on the icon you are presented with the mail messages waiting. Double-clicking brings up the message. Enclosures such as extra files can be added to the message by the sender, as shown by the icon in the top left of the window. You can reply to the message simply by pressing the Reply button on the right and typing your reply in the text window which appears.

135

The glory of AppleLink is that it looks and feels like your Mac.

4 By double-clicking on a conference you are interested in, you are presented with the contents of the conference. Double-click again to bring up different windows. For example, there is a shareware area from which you can download software utilities for use with PowerBooks.

Finding Out More

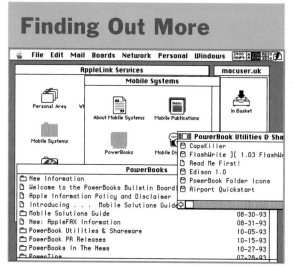

There are many Mac areas on AppleLink – this is PowerBook.

5 You enter a support forum in the same way, but here people post messages about problems they are having or solutions they have found. This query has been given a reply by another user. You can also reply by clicking in the Reply button.

Send and receive information to help you with your Mac-life.

USER GROUPS

If you are still unsure about all this 'logging-on', 'downloading', 'uploading' stuff; and if plugging your Mac into a telephone socket fills you with horror, then you might like to meet some fellow Mac users face-to-face in order to chat about problems, and of course, to come up with some solutions.

If this is the case, then user groups are a good meeting place to share problems and compare notes about using your Mac.

User groups range from gatherings of amateur enthusiasts who meet regularly in your local area to commercial organizations like the Macintosh Association in the UK, which publishes its own user magazine MacTimes, and the large US groups like BMUG which actually began the whole user group experience way back in the dim-distant past.

As well as being meeting places, some user groups will keep shareware collections that you can access for free, and also run special interest groups about, for instance, graphics or databases. Some organizations make a small charge to join, while others, usually local small groups, are free. Either way, user groups are an ideal way in which to rid yourself of any remaining techno-fear that you might have – and this will mean that your Mac useage will be more productive and more fun.

RTFM

This stands for 'Read The "Friendly" Manual', a saying which, if you consider some of the thick, complex and techno-filled 'manuals' that come with software and some third-party software, can be an oxymoron!

That aside, manuals do provide a wealth of information about the products you have bought. Most software programs come with tutorial guides to walk you through specific examples of how to create certain kinds of documents. The good ones also come with booklets or single cards (called Quick Start Guides) that tell you about getting started and give you the basics of how to use the hardware and software.

The reference manual should detail every command in the program and what it is for. Mac manuals tend to be better written and presented than their PC counterparts, which makes them easier to get round, but they do often assume a level of knowledge which many beginners do not have.

If you still can't get any joy… call the manufacturers.

IF ALL ELSE FAILS

Many people are worried about doing this; don't be. The good thing about the Macintosh world is that the vast majority of dealers and developers set a very high standard both for their products and for their support. So if you get into hot water, or just cannot understand what is supposed to be going on… make that call and ask for help.

There are a number of Mac magazines available to you:

MAGAZINES

These are general US Mac magazines:

MACUSER (monthly):
Subscriptions 303 447 9330).

MACWORLD (monthly):
(Subscriptions 415 267 1743).

MACWEEK (weekly): Subscription-only
industry newspaper. Indispensable for
developers and business buyers.
(Subscriptions 609 461 2100).

MACHOME JOURNAL (monthly):
Home user and small business magazine.
(Subscriptions 415 957 1911).

These are European titles (available on
subscription to the USA)

MACUSER UK (fortnightly): Europe's leading
Mac magazine covers new product news
and reviews, comparison reports on
hardware and software, and advice
sections. (Subscriptions +011 44 454
620070).

MACWORLD (monthly): UK sister of US
Macworld, covering new product reviews
and news, buying reports and advice.
Some content is localized for the UK from
the US *Macworld*. (Subscriptions +011
44 71 831 9252).

THE MAC (monthly): Aimed at new users and
the consumer market, with new product
reviews, advice features and large games
and CD-ROM sections. (Subscriptions
+011 44 454 620070).

MACFORMAT (monthly): Aimed at new
users, with advice, features and reviews.
(Subscriptions +011 44 458 74011).

WHERE TO BUY

● *High Street Stores:* high street retailers are
now selling Performas alongside dodgy videos and
cheap cameras. Pricing is competitive but expertise
is limited.
Verdict: know exactly what you want to buy.
Don't tell them you're 'looking for a cheap
computer' – they'll try to sell you a PC.

● *Value-Added Resellers:* experienced in
providing solutions to problems by selling you a
whole set-up in one go.
Verdict: Cheaper to buy your bits separately from
the cheapest outlets.

● *Mail Order:* maligned reputation which is
undeserved by the professional mail order
operations.
Verdict: Cheap source of products. Order through
advertising in Mac magazines that offer support
mail order protection schemes (also use a credit
card for insurance protection).

● *Secondhand:* There's a healthy second-hand
market for Mac hardware, but prices tend to be
unrealistic. Selling secondhand software is illegal;
buying it is merely stupid.
Verdict: Macs are reliable but there's no such
thing as 'one' careful owner.

Keywords

Accelerator board

A board or card slotted into a Mac to boost general performance or speed up specific operations – for example, graphics.

Access

To find, open or use a file or any part of your Mac set up. If you can't access a printer, you won't be able to print.

ADB

(Apple Desktop Bus.) An Appledevloped system of connecting hardware to your Mac (most commonly used for keyboards or mice).

Alias

A small (1-2K) icon pointing the way to a document or application. Aliases are pointers, not copies of applications. Use them for convenient access or to group projects. Don't purge the single original, though. To make an, Alias select the target, then choose Make Alias from the File menu in the Finder.

Apple Menu

The menu under the Apple logo at the far left of the screen. Anything you choose to place in the Apple menu is easily accessible at all times.

Appletalk

A software networking system that links Macs together.

Application

A program that provides the means to achieve a specific task – for example, a word processor, or a DTP package.

ATM

Adobe Type Manager is a small program from Adobe which enables the Mac to display PostScript fonts smoothly on screen at any size – whether or not you hold the screen fonts. ATM also enables PostScript fonts to be printed to non-PostScript printers.

Backup

A copy of your original work.

Balloon Help

On-screen help. Find it to the right on the Desktop menu bar.

Baud

Bauds are a measure of data speed, often referred to in the context of modems. A high baud rate means a fast modem.

BBS

See Bulletin Board

Beta software

Software in the late stages of development.

Bit

BInary digITs (1 and 0) : the smallest amount of data a computer can handle. There are 8 bits to a Byte.

Bitmap

An image made up of individual dots that are either on or off. All output devices are bitmap devices – the resolution or number of dots crammed into a specific area is what determines the quality of the output. Bitmap images are not scalable so a bitmap image produced on a 72 dots per inch computer screen will still only have this number of dots (but blown up) when printed to a 300dpi printer.

Boot (Boot-up)

Start up the Mac.

Bug

An error in the application causing it to crash. Sometimes affects the program in use, sometimes crashes the whole Mac, which will then have to be restarted.

Bulletin Board

A public area on-line, area where you can leave and receive messages and swap information. To get onto a bulletin board you'll need a modem, the right software and a phone line.

Bus

The circuits that carry information from one part of your Mac to another. The Mac uses a standard called NuBus.

CD–ROM

Compact Disc Read-Only Memory. CD–ROMs are discs that can be used to store up to 650 megabytes of data. Accessed on a Mac via a CD-ROM drive, CD-ROMS look much like normal hard disks. The difference is that data access is slower and that data cannot be written to the CD-ROMs from the Mac (hence they are read only).

Chip

A small piece of silicon with circuits printed onto it. The basic building blocks of computers.

Chooser

A desk accessory accessible via the Apple Menu. Used for choosing printers (or file servers if Macs are connected together).

Clipboard

A temporary storage area in your Mac. This holds the last chunk of information you copied or cut. Pasted information comes from the clipboard. The Scrapbook performs the same function but can hold images long term.

Close

Close a document and you leave the application running. (See Quit.)

CMYK

Cyan, Magenta, Yellow and Black (Key). A color system used by printers which doesn't exactly match the Mac Red Green Blue system. This is why screen color won't look exactly like printed color.

Command Key

The key with the Apple and curly four-leaf clover symbol. It's used to give commands in conjunction with other keys. For example, Command-Q is Quit in many applications.

Compression

The reduction of the amount of space that data takes up on a Mac. Lossless data compression means you can re-expand a file to its original quality. Lossy compression means some data is lost on re-expansion – often used for images where this may not be crucial.

Control Panels

A series of panels controlling different aspects of the Mac interface. Held in the System Folder, but you can access them under the Apple menu. Keyboards, monitors, mouse, and color settings can all be adjusted using control panels.

Copy

A command under the Edit menu of almost all applications and in the Finder. Will copy selected text or objects onto the Mac's clipboard where they can be Pasted to a new location. Also a duplicate of a file.

CPU

Central Processing Unit. The heart of the Mac – the chip that does most of the work. The Mac CPU is based on Motorola 680X0 chips.

Crash

Stop working after software failure. The screen will freeze or you see a bomb on the screen. Either way you probably have to restart.

Cut

Deletes a selected object from one place and puts it on the clipboard ready to be placed elsewhere.

Database

Strictly a set of related data - say addresses or product information. It also tends to refer to database applications - like *FileMaker Pro*.

Defragment
An action carried out by software that ensures that the data on your hard disk is stored in a concurrent manner, rather than being scattered all over the disk. Regular defragmenting with a program such as *Norton Utilities* will retain your Mac's speed and efficiency.

Dingbats
Characters in a typeface that don't fit into the alphabet – for example, bullet points or arrows. There's a typeface called Zapf Dingbats entirely composed of these.

Double click
Click twice on the mouse. Click once to select; double click to make your Mac act on the selection.

Download
Copy – for example, you download files from a bulletin board to a Mac or download fonts from a Mac to a printer.

Dpi
Dots per inch. A way of measuring the quality of a scanner or printer, it describes the number of dots packed into a certain area. The higher the dpi the higher the image resolution.

Drivers
A driver is a piece of software which tells your Mac how to communicate with external hardware. Printers and external hard drives have drivers - you can find them in the system folder.

Drives
Drives are the mechanisms that handle floppy or hard disks. Virtually all Macs have internal hard drives and a floppy drive slot where you insert floppy disks. The drive spins them so the information they hold can be accessed.

DTP
Desktop Publishing. Combining text and graphics to publish a document.

Email
Electronic Mail sent from Mac to Mac or via a bulletin board service.

Emulation
If one operating system - say the Mac's - can emulate another it can run software from that platform. There is emulation software to run PC-Windows applications on the Mac.

EPS
Encapsulated PostScript – a high quality page description language that is used to handle graphics files.

Fax modem
A modem and fax machine combined so Mac files can be transmitted and faxes received. Some fax modems can receive files too.

File format
The way in which a file is stored. This may be very different from application to application. Standard file formats include ASCII(text), EPS and TIFF(graphics).

File
A piece of information stored on a Mac – applications, work documents and system items are all files.

Finder
The program that creates the desktop you see when you open a Mac and which enables files to be accessed and managed.

Font
A font is a variation on a typface. For example, Times is a typeface but Times Italic (*Times*) is a font.

Floppy
A 3.5-in disk that holds 800K or 1.4Mb of data – depending whether it's standard or double density. The floppy disk itself is encased in rigid plastic.

FPU
Floating Point Unit – or maths co-processor. A chip that speeds up maths-intensive jobs such as spreadsheets or graphics.

Get Info
Basic information on files or folders Access it via the File menu on the desktop.

Gigabyte (Gb)
A unit of measurement.A gigabyte is 1,024 megabytes - a single file this large would be enormous,but gigabyte disk drives are becoming slightly more common.

Hackers
Hacking into someone else's computer or their files means gaining unauthorised entry.

Hard disk
Internal or external storage medium for files or applications. Capacity ranges from 20 megabytes up.

Icon
A pictorial representation of an object – including an application, document, file or hard or floppy disk.

Imagesetter
A high resolution output device.

Initialize
Initializing a disk means formatting it so the Mac can use it to read and write to it.

INIT
A program that needs to be placed in the Extensions Folder in the System Folder of a Mac to work. INITS are often small programs that run peripheral devices such as printers or scanners.

JPEG
A widely used still-image compression standard. Stands for Joint Photographic Experts Group.

Kerning
Closing up spaces between pairs of letters (for example AV or A V) so they look better together.

Keyboard shortcut
Using the keyboard to do certain jobs. For example Command-Q is normally Quit.

Leading *(Pronounced 'Led-ing')*
The amount of space between two lines of type – derives from hot metal printing when blocks of lead (called slugs) were used to separate lines of text.

Launch
To open or start an application.

Lock
To restrict access to a disk or file.

Macros
A string of commands all activated by pressing one key or a combination of keys. Some programs, such as Microsoft *Word* and *ClarisWorks* include macros that work by watching what you do.

Megabyte (Mb or M)
Defines the capacity of storage systems – whether these are RAM or magnetic media like disk or tape.

Modem
MODulator, DEModulator. Modems transform digital information from computers into analogue signals that can be sent on public phone lines.

Multimedia
The integration of elements including text and graphics and time based media like video and sound.

NTSC
US TV standard.

NuBus

A connection system standard across different Macs. A NuBus card can be 'slotted' into compatible Macs and should work identically. NuBus cards are used for adding extra monitor support, or for accelerators or video grabbing.

PAL

UK TV standard.

Paste

Placing an object from the clipboard onto a selected area.

PDA

Personal Digital Assistant such as the Apple Newton that can talk to Macs.

PDL

Page Description Language. A way of controlling an output device by sending a coded description of an image which is then rasterized into a bitmap. (See rasterize, bitmap.).

PICT

A graphics file format for PICTures.

Pixel

PixElement – or Picture Element – The smallest dot on a Mac display that can be controlled. The greater the pixels per inch, the higher the resolution of the display. Equates to dpi on printers and monitors. Most Macs display at 72 dpi.

Point

A typesetting measure. Equals 1/72nd of an inch.

Port

A socket connecting your Mac to the outside world.

PostScript

The most popular Page Description Language and a standard for publishing professionals.

Preferences

User definable settings for customizing applications and programs.

QuickDraw

Controls how the Mac draws graphics and text on screen. It can also be used to output to devices that are not PostScript.

QuickTime

A system extension that is the Mac's standard format for storing and playing moving images and sound.

Quit

Quitting means leaving an application completely, rather than simply closing a document within it.

RAM

Random Access Memory – chips used to store data temporarily. Data held in RAM is lost if power is switched off, so data must be saved to a device like a hard disk for secure storage.

Rasterize

The process of converting a page description (held in code) into a bitmap (dot) image. (See also PDL and Bitmap.)

RGB

Red, Green, Blue. A form of specifying color on monitors.

RIP

Raster Image Processor – a device to convert a PostScript file into a bitmap. Laser printers tend to have these built in.

ROM

Read Only Memory. Normally refers to the chips inside a Mac that hold parts of the operating system.

Scrapbook

A desk accessory (find it under the Apple menu) for storing images or blocks of text for re-use.

SCSI

Small Computer System Interface. A standard way of connecting devices to a Mac. Up to eight devices can be daisy chained together. Pronounce it 'Scuzzy'.

Shareware

Try-before-you-buy software. Can be freely distributed, but if you like it, you send money to the author.

SIMM

(Single Inline Memory Module(Memory chips. Used to expand the memory of your Mac. Often referred to simply as RAM.

StartUp Disk

The disk that holds the system software the Mac needs to start up – normally your internal hard drive.

System Folder

The folder holding the system software used to run a Mac. Symbolized by a small Mac within the folder.

TeachText

Basic word processing application that arrives with your Mac.

TrueType

An font format. TrueType fonts are scalable so they appear smooth at any size and on any output device.

TIFF

Tagged Image File Format: Graphics format – useful for scanned images.

Undo

Undoes the last thing you did – if you're lucky.

Utility

A small application that can handle one or two functions.

Video card

A piece of hardware that controls the quality of the display on a screen. Different cards can provide different numbers of colours.

Virus

A program designed to spread illegally from computer to computer. Some are harmless; some can corrupt data. Make sure you get some anti-virus software – for example, *Disinfectant*.

WYSIWYG

What You See Is What You Get - the fact that what you see on your screen will, roughly, translate to what you see when you print it out.

ZZZZZZ

After a hard day's computing…

Index

143

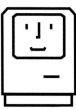